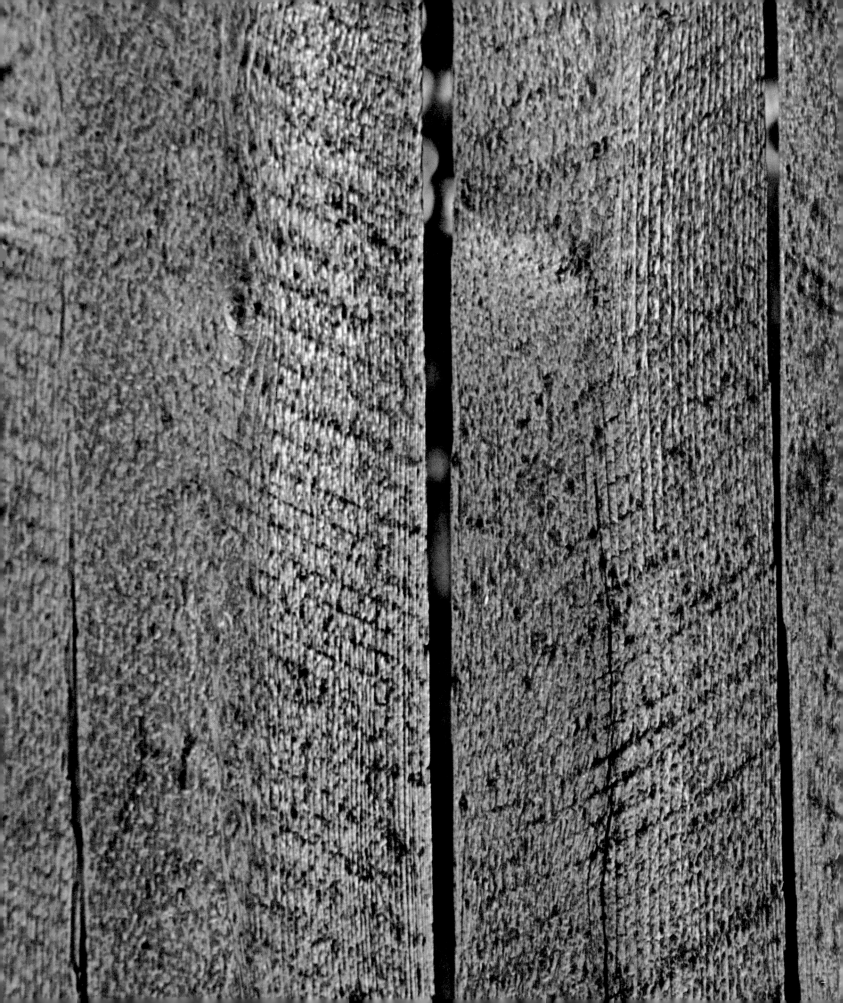

THE FAMILY
CREATIVE WORKSHOP

4

Carryalls, Cartooning, Carving, Casting,
Ceramics, Cheeses and Churning,
Christmas Celebrations, Clambakes,
Collages and Assemblages,
Colonial Crafts, Color Psychology,
Confections and Comfits

Plenary Publications International, Inc.
New York and Amsterdam

The Project-Evaluation Symbols appearing in the title heading at the beginning of each project have these meanings:

Range of approximate cost:

¢ Low: Under $5, or free and found natural materials

$ Medium: About $10

$$ High: Above $15

Estimated time to completion for an unskilled adult:

⊠ Hours

● Days

 Weeks

Suggested level of experience:

Child alone

Supervised child or family project

Unskilled adult

Specialized prior training

Tools and equipment:

Small hand tools

Large hand and household tools

Specialized or powered equipment

Publishers
Plenary Publications International, Incorporated, 10 East 49th Street, New York, N.Y. 10017

Jerry Curcio, Production Manager
Nancy Jackson, Administrative Assistant

Originating Editor of the series:
Allen Davenport Bragdon

Editorial Preparation
Wentworth Press, Incorporated

Walter Ian Fischman, Director.
Jacqueline Heriteau, Editor.
Francesca Morris, Executive Editor.
Susan Lusk, Art Director.
Frank Lusk, Director of Photography.
Maxine Krasnow, Production Manager.

For this volume
Contributing editors: Betsy Barley, Jo-Anne Jarrin, Veronica McNiff, Molli Nickell, John Noblitt, John Savage, Lari Siler, Jane Miller.

Contributing illustrators: Mark Drucker, Peter Kalberkamp, Maggie MacGowan.

Contributing photographers: Lionel Freedman, J. Alan Brzys, Harvey W. Friedman, Nancy Jackson, Eric Koniger, Laszlo, Stephen McCarroll, Susan Meiselas, John Savage, Melissa Schnirring.

Ceramic-glaze chart, Ceramics, courtesy of San Diego State University. Christmas-tree toys, Christmas Celebrations, courtesy of the Horticulture Design Group. Photographs, Colonial Crafts, taken at Old Sturbridge Village, Massachusetts, where village life of the period has been faithfully restored. Color Psychology photographs: Farnsworth-Munsell color-defective-vision tests, courtesy of Dr. Alan Lewis, Optometric Center of New York; mosaic of the Emperor Justinian, courtesy of Scala New York/Florence. Confections and Comfits recipes tested and photographed in the Kitchens of Karo Corn Syrup, Best Foods.

On the cover:
Clay tiles are rolled, cut, glazed and decorated to your own specifications before firing them for strength and durability. See "Ceramics", page 434.
Photograph by Paul Levin.

Published by Plenary Publications International Incorporated, 10 East 49th Street, New York, N.Y. 10017, for the Blue Mountain Crafts Council.

Library of Congress Catalog Card Number: 73-89331
Complete set International Standard Book Number: 0-88459-021-6. Volume 4 International Standard Book Number: 0-88459-003-8.

Manufactured in the United States of America.
Printed and bound by the W. A. Krueger Company. Brookfield, Wisconsin.
Color separations by Lithotech, Incorporated, Orlando, Florida.

Contents

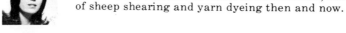

Totes and Bags To Make

John Brucciani is an award-winning leathercrafter who works in a New York City suburb. Originally an engineer, he opened his own shop in Nyack, N.Y., where he makes and sells crafted leather goods and teaches students and apprentices. Brucciani's many awards include prizes from craft shows in the New England area.

The carryall is a symbol of our age. We live at an accelerated pace and are on the move more than we ever were in earlier years. Because we are so mobile, we are almost always in need of an efficient, comfortable container for our belongings. Leather, canvas, and vinyl carryalls fill this need admirably and are easy to make.

Of the three materials, leather is the sturdiest. Because it has no weave, it withstands maximum stress. Canvas has proved its resistance to rough wear through years of sailing applications. Vinyl is a modern, pliable plastic. Clear vinyl tears easily, but when bonded to a layer of foam or cloth backing, it becomes quite sturdy. An advantage of vinyl is that it can be kept clean simply by wiping it with soap and water. Leather has a porous surface, which must be periodically cleaned and oiled. Canvas needs to be washed by machine fairly frequently.

The tote-bag, back pack, feed bag, and duffel bag described on the following pages can be made with leather, canvas, or vinyl. I have made the tote of vinyl, the back pack of canvas, and the feed bag and duffel bag of leather, so techniques for working with each of these materials are described on the following pages. You can, using the patterns and instructions for a project—the tote bag, for instance—make that carryall from either of the other two materials.

Special tools for working with leather and leatherlike materials are shown in the Craftnotes section, page 400, along with detailed drawings of leatherworking techniques useful for the projects in which leather or vinyl is used. A careful study of the Craftnotes before you undertake vinyl or leather projects is recommended.

Canvas and vinyl can be purchased in many fabric stores. They are sold by the yard in a variety of weights, textures, and colors. Leather can be ordered from a tanner or purchased in smaller amounts from a commercial leather shop. (See Leather Craftnotes on page 52, Volume One.)

Tools and Materials

In addition to the leather, canvas, or vinyl, the basic tools and materials you will need for these projects include the following items:

Patternmaking Paper: Brown wrapping paper is a good substitute.

Masking Tape: For securing patterns to leather, canvas, or vinyl. Cellophane tape will also work.

Shears: A good, sharp pair for clean cutting.

Straightedge: A metal ruler for measuring and for exact marking of pattern. Wooden rulers are easily displaced as you work and can result in lines which are not straight.

Grease Pencil: For tracing patterns on vinyl surfaces. Or use tailor's chalk.

Rubber Cement: For temporary "basting" prior to hand or machine sewing.

Awl: For puncturing holes in leather. It should be quite sharp. A carpenter's awl works well.

Hammer or Mallet: For flattening seams in vinyl and leather. I often use a cobbler's hammer, because it works well for me; but any type of round-headed hammer will do. A really new metal hammer, used too vigorously, could mark leather and should be covered with a couple of thicknesses of nylon or cheesecloth to soften its hitting surface.

A back pack is one of the most useful of modern totes. Made of durable canvas, it will last through a lifetime of travel and is surprisingly easy to make. Instructions for making this one begin on page 395. It can also be made of leather.

Needlecrafts
Vinyl tote bag

$ ☒ ⚊ ✀

To make the vinyl tote bag pictured on the facing page, you will need 1½ yards of cloth-backed, medium-weight vinyl in 54-inch width, a size-14 needle for your sewing machine, and size-50 mercerized thread.

Enlarge and cut out pattern pieces, figure B; cut two handles. With masking tape, secure pattern to the wrong side (back) of vinyl; with grease pencil, trace pattern, and transfer all pattern markings. Cut along solid cutting lines of pattern. Set stitch-length selector of your sewing machine at 8 or 10, and test stitch two layers of scrap vinyl to adjust thread tension on the machine. (You can also handsew the tote, using size-50 mercerized thread smoothed with beeswax and a large embroidery needle.)

Cut out triangles at the base of the tote as shown in photograph 2, and glue and fold top edges together as in photographs 3 and 4.

A

Figure A: With tailor's chalk or grease pencil, transfer markings from pattern, figure B, to vinyl. This detail shows a square with an X, which indicates sewing lines for joining handle end to bag.

1: A straightedge ruler is used in drawing a pattern precisely on vinyl. Be sure the work is well lighted, especially when you are making small adjustments.

392   2: Cut in on the lines that form the triangles at the base of the tote. Remove these two triangles of vinyl. The flaps will later be handsewn to the outside of the tote bottom.

3: With a brush, apply a coat of rubber cement to top 4 inches of the bag on the wrong (back) side. Let rubber cement dry completely (about a minute) so surfaces will adhere firmly when pressed together.

4: Fold top 2 inches over onto bottom 2 inches of rubber-cement-coated vinyl, wrong sides together. Press down firmly along fold line for top of tote. This makes a finished top edge for the bag.

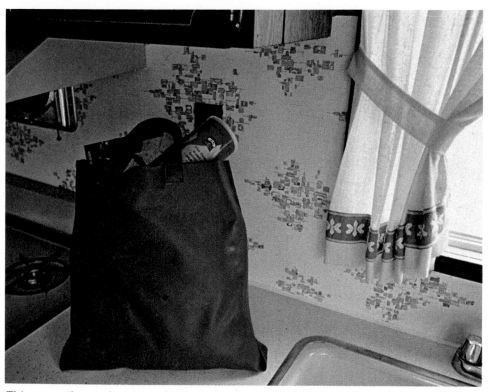

This versatile tote bag is made of vinyl, cut as a single piece and glued and stitched in a very simple operation. You can also make it of leather or canvas.

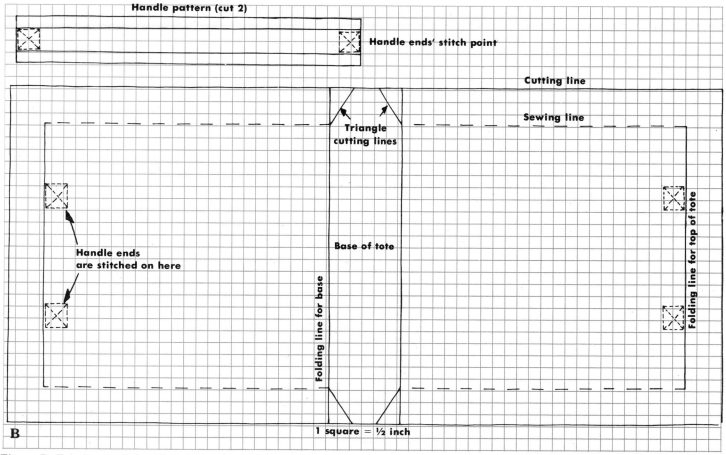

Figure B: Tote-bag pattern. To enlarge, for each square draw ½-inch square on pattern paper, as described on page 57, Volume One.

Joining the Tote Sides

Fold tote so right (face) sides are together, and align glued edges. On the wrong side, stitch the seam along the dashed sewing lines on the pattern from the top of one glued edge to a few stitches short of the bottom corner (see photograph 5). Stitch other side the same way. Leave long threads at seam ends; pull them to inside of the bag; knot two or three times; cut off.

Turn the bag right side out. With size-50 mercerized thread, beeswaxed, and a large embroidery or leatherworking needle (see Craftnotes, page 400), hand baste both corners. Be sure corner-flap triangle is on the outside (photograph 6). At last stitch, push needle to inside; pull thread through.

With needle and thread inside, turn the bag inside out; take three stitches on the same spot to secure the thread; then cut it.

Attaching the Handles

Follow these instructions for making and attaching each handle:

With handle piece right (face) side down on your worktable, brush entire surface with a light coat of rubber cement, and let it dry completely.

Along fold lines indicated on pattern, figure B, page 393, fold side edges inward. They should meet in the center to give handles a neat finish. Press down firmly to flatten glued pieces. Handle is now ready to be attached.

Handle ends are affixed by stitching a square and an X within it, as in figures A and B, pages 392, 393. Match squares and X's of handle end and bag; then place the seamed (wrong side) of handle end to the X'd square on the right (face) side of bag, and stitch a large X in the square at this place (photograph 8). Making sure the handle is not twisted, attach the other end to the same side of the bag, at the other point marked with an X'd square.

Attach the second handle to the other side of the bag the same way.

5: Stitch the side seams together with a sewing machine. Use a seam guide to keep a uniform seam width as you sew. Sew at a slow pace to avoid pulling the vinyl.

6: Hand baste the bottom seam with the tote right side out and the flaps on the outside. Use double thread. Pull needle through with pliers if necessary.

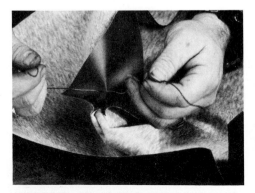

7: Finish hand stitching with tote turned inside out and triangle flaps still on outside. Tie two or three firm knots; then snip off thread close to the vinyl.

8: Attach handles to sides of tote. When stitching is finished at each end, leave long threads, and pull these through to inside of tote. Knot thread; trim excess.

Needlecrafts
Canvas back pack

$ X 🚶 🧵

This canvas back pack, pictured on page 391 and below, right, uses the basic techniques described in the previous section. Two side panels (see pattern, figure C) make it roomier than the tote, and the large flap protects its contents. You will need 1¾ yards of medium-weight canvas and a heavy-duty snap or buckle fastener. Test your machine to make sure it can handle heavy canvas. Adjust and test stitch length and thread tension as for vinyl. Always press along fold lines with an iron before sewing.

Follow procedures in preceding section to prepare the pattern and cut out fabric. Cut two pieces of both strap and back-pack side patterns Adjust strap length to suit your size—shorten or lengthen if necessary.

Fold, press, then sew straps along dotted lines. Attach straps at X'd squares on strap ends to X'd squares on back-pack pattern, as in preceding section and photograph 9. Fold, press, then stitch flap edges at top of back pack along inner solid line. Tie off threads.

Follow these instructions to attach each of the side pieces to back pack:

Match dots on side pieces to dots on back-pack pattern. On wrong side, stitch panel to pack from dot to dot. Then continue stitching side piece to pack along dashed seam lines, to right and to left of dots, until three edges are joined. Join second side piece the same way. Then, with the inside out, top stitch all seams.

Attach buckle or snap to flap edge and to pack. Then trim threads and any excess length on the straps, as shown in photograph 10.

Consuela English, a high school student in Chappaqua, N.Y., designed the canvas back pack below. As a major in visual arts, she enjoys designing and sewing clothing and accessories.

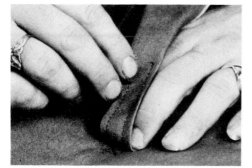

9: Place X'd square on strap end over X'd square on canvas. Machine stitch to join.

10: A neat appearance results from careful trimming of straps and threads.

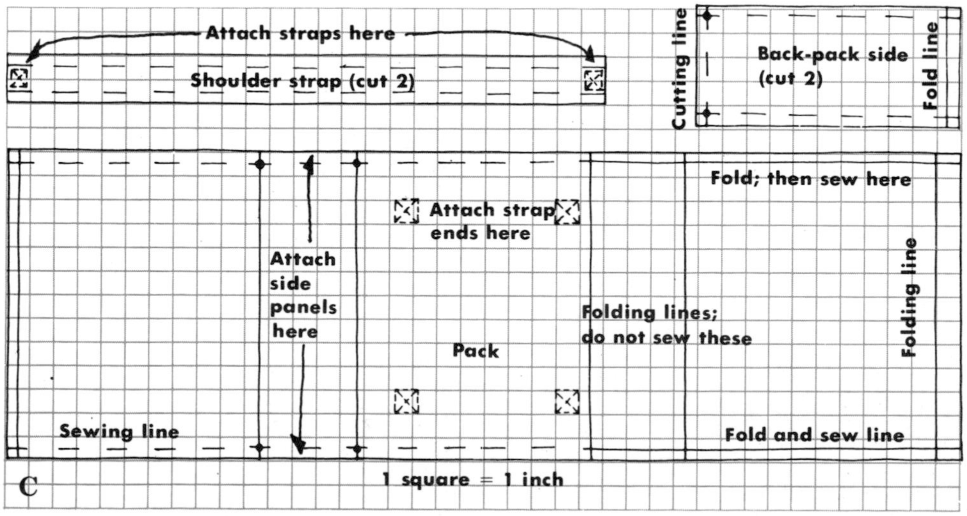

Back pack, popular teen carryall, is made from 1¾ yards of canvas. Books and clothing can be easily carried inside, and hands are left free.

Figure C: Pattern for back pack.

[Pattern diagram labels:]
Attach straps here
Shoulder strap (cut 2)
Cutting line
Back-pack side (cut 2)
Fold line
Fold; then sew here
Attach strap ends here
Attach side panels here
Folding line
Folding lines; do not sew these
Pack
Sewing line
Fold and sew line
C
1 square = 1 inch

Leathercrafts
Feed-bag carryalls

$ 🗙 👤 🧵

This tote is in the shape of a feed bag. To make it, you will need 2½ square feet of chrome-tanned, lightweight garment leather, four medium-size rivets with ¼-inch posts, five brass rings of 1-inch diameter, a brass dog-leash clasp, four-ply nylon thread, and, if you are sewing by machine, a size 19 or 20 needle. If you are handsewing, use one of the needles shown in the Craftnotes, page 400, and the same weight thread, coated with beeswax. Or hand lace with ⅛-inch leather thong, as instructed in the Craftnotes.

On cardboard, enlarge the three pattern pieces, figure D, page 398. Use shears to cut out one of each of the pattern pieces.

Place the cardboard pattern pieces on the wrong side of the leather, as shown in photograph 11. Hold them in place with tape, and trace around them with grease pencil. Cut cleanly with sharp shears.

Apply rubber cement to both sides of bag, as shown in photograph 12. When cement is dry, press together to hold for stitching.

Stitch this seam, by hand or by machine. If you are using a machine, sew

11: Trace cardboard pattern pieces on back of leather. Start by penciling key line for main pattern piece; then tape down, and trace the pattern.

12: Put rubber cement on right (smooth) side along stitching line at one end of tote and on wrong side at the other end. Let dry. Press ends together. Stitch.

13: Flattening opened-out, glued-down, seam-allowance edges with a hammer. You can use a cobbler's hammer, as here, or a wooden mallet.

▶Feed-bag carryalls can be used to hold everything from groceries to—feed. Made of durable leather, this one will withstand years of rough wear and tear.

14: Brush rubber cement on face (right) side of the bottom circle. Cement must be evenly distributed all around the edge of the circle, in a band ½ inch wide.

15: With the cylindrical bag inside out, press the bottom piece firmly to the rubber-cemented bottom edge of the right side of the cylinder.

16: Stitch glued circular seam, as close to the edge as possible. If you prefer to make this seam with leather lacing, refer to Craftnotes, page 400.

17: Pound the sides of the shoulder strap flat, with a hammer, after rubber cement has dried. The strap should now be about 1 inch wide.

18: Pull one end of the shoulder strap through the ring of dog-leash clasp. Only 1 inch of the strap should loop through. The end will be secured with two rivets.

19: Hammer rivets to close strap end around the clasp. Rivet holes can be made with awl and hammer, or a rotary-wheel punch (see Craftnotes, page 400).

very slowly to avoid damaging the leather. If necessary, turn the motor wheel by hand to control the speed of the machine. You now have a cylinder.

Open the seam allowance flat by pulling edges apart. Apply rubber cement to undersides of seam-allowance edges and to leather directly beneath them. Let dry. Press down, and flatten with a hammer, as shown in photograph 13. See also Craftnotes, page 400, for details of this step.

Apply rubber cement to the edge of the circular bottom piece, as shown in photograph 14. Then apply a ½-inch band of rubber cement to the bottom edge of the right side of the now-cylindrical piece. Let dry. Press cemented edges together, as shown in photograph 15. Stitch this seam by hand or by machine (photograph 16). Finish the top edge of the cylinder by turning down 1 inch along fold line and stitching.

Brush cement over the wrong side of the strap piece. Turn both sides of strap piece in to the middle, along fold lines. Press; let dry; pound flat, as in photograph 17. Pull one strap end through the ring of the dog-leash clasp (photograph 18). Make a loop, and fasten loop with two rivets. To install rivets, see Craftnotes with the entry "Belts and Buckles," Volume Two.

With a rotary-wheel punch or an awl, punch four holes, marked on pattern piece, at top of bag; put brass rings through these holes (see photographs 20 and 21, page 398). With an awl and a hammer, make two holes, as noted on pattern, near the bag's bottom, close to the seam: Make first hole; fold fabric in half, along seam; place awl through first hole, and hammer it through the other side. Put a brass ring through both holes. Loop free end of strap through bottom brass ring. See photographs 22 and 23, page 398.

Attach the dog-leash clasp to the five brass rings at the top of the bag to close it, as shown in photograph 24, page 398.

20: With rotary-wheel punch, make four equidistant holes around the top of bag. Awl and mallet can be used instead.

21: Place brass rings through holes. When rings are in place, tighten them securely with pliers.

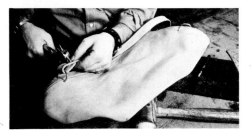

22: Make holes for ring near bottom of bag, using awl and mallet or hammer. Wood block inside protects other side.

23: Use rotary-wheel punch to make holes for rivets on bottom of the strap, after strap has been closed around ring.

24: To close the feed-bag tote, snap the dog-leash clasp through the four brass rings at the top of the bag.

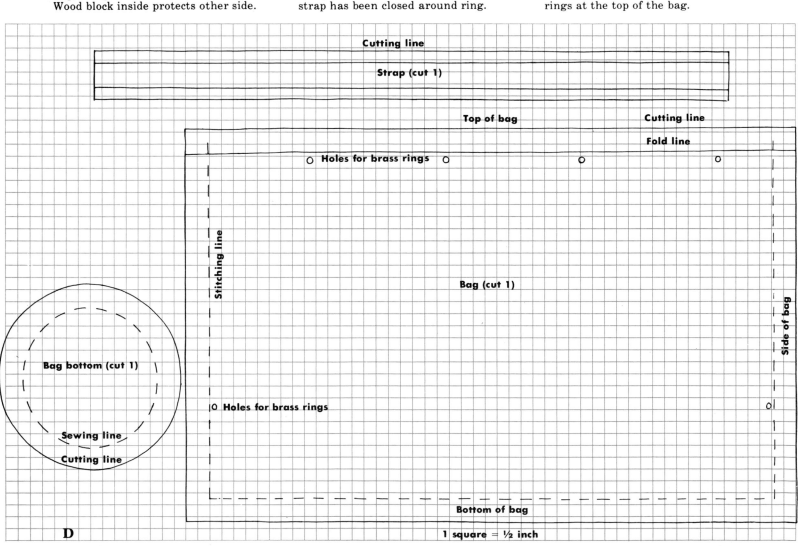

Cutting line

Strap (cut 1)

Top of bag

Cutting line

Fold line

o Holes for brass rings o   o   o

Stitching line

Bag (cut 1)

Side of bag

Bag bottom (cut 1)

Sewing line

Cutting line

|0 Holes for brass rings

Bottom of bag

1 square = ½ inch

D

Figure D: Pattern for feed bag. Cut out one of each piece: rectangle, circle, strap.

Duffel Bag

This duffel bag is a variation of the shoulder feed bag. Use pattern, figure E. You need 3 square feet of leather. Follow instructions for previous projects, with these differences: leave an 18-inch opening between dots on pattern in center of side seam. Using backstitch, attach an 18-inch zipper. See the Craftnotes, page 401.

Attach the second circle at the other end of the cylinder. Add two leather handles at X'd squares, one on each side of zipper.

For related projects, see "Basketry," and "Leatherworking."

25: Zipper is sewn into 18-inch opening left between dots on seam allowance (dashed line of pattern). Before stitching, glue down seam allowances of zipper opening, and tape zipper into place, as shown in Craftnotes, page 401.

26: Attach handles to the bag, one on each side of the zipper opening at the squares marked with Xs. These may be hand or machine stitched. Be sure that the stitching is well done and the handles are firmly attached.

The duffel bag is a welcome companion on any short trip. It is made much the same as the feed-bag tote, but is closed at both ends and has a side zipper and two straps.

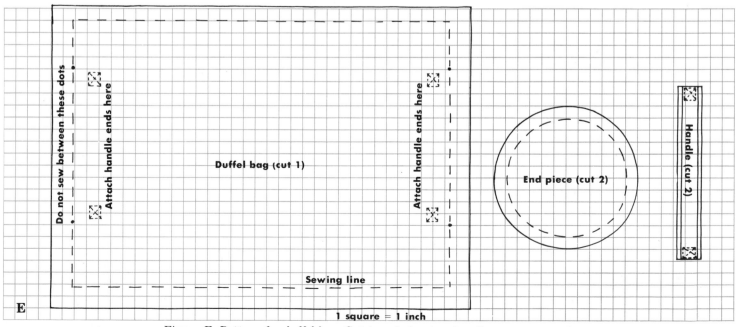

Do not sew between these dots

Attach handle ends here

Duffel bag (cut 1)

Attach handle ends here

End piece (cut 2)

Handle (cut 2)

Sewing line

1 square = 1 inch

E

Figure E: Pattern for duffel bag. Cut two circles, two handles, one rectangle.

LEATHER

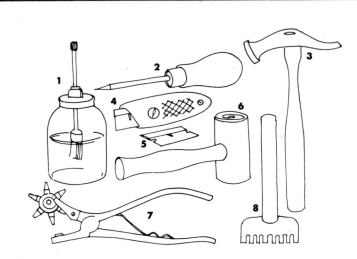

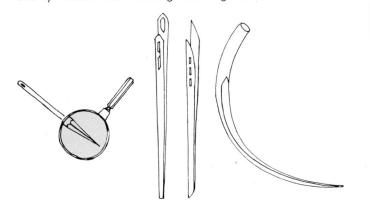

Most common leather-lacing needles, below, left to right: glover's needle, hook-and-eye needle, two-prong split needle, life-eye needle. The glover's needle is triangular in cross section, as magnified detail shows. Very sharp, it is used for sewing through leather without first punching holes. The other three needles are for lacing through holes. Lacing can be threaded through the hook-and-eye needle, whereas the two-prong split needle merely grips the end of lacing. Life-eye needle aids in sewing hard-to-get-at corners.

Leathercrafter's basic tool kit: (1) rubber-cement jar with brush; (2) awl; (3) cobbler's hammer; (4) straightedge craft knife; (5) single-edge razor blade; (6) shoemaker's leather or rubber mallet; (7) rotary leather punch; (8) thonging chisel. Mallet, rotary leather punch, and thonging chisel can be purchased in craft shops and usually are available where leather supplies are sold.

Hints on leather lacing: To lace a leather seam without a glover's needle (right) make holes in the leather large enough to accommodate lacing. The rotary leather punch makes one hole at a time. Select hole size; insert leather; squeeze handle. Space holes evenly over seam line.

The thonging chisel makes a series of small, evenly spaced slits and may be used as an alternate to the rotary punch. Place point of chisel on face side of leather. With a mallet, pound chisel into leather until slit is made. Continue along seam line until you have an evenly spaced line of small slits. Then stitch seam, passing lacing through holes (or slits) as shown in diagrams on opposite page.

When seam is sewn and ends of lacing are secured, sides of seam may be pounded flat with a mallet. Follow instructions and drawings on the opposite page.

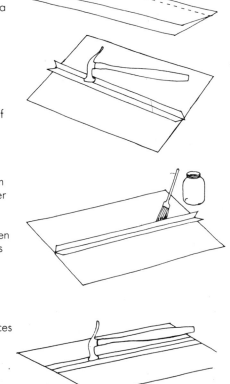

Pounding leather seams: Once you have sewn a seam in leather, you must flatten its sides. Working on the wrong side, open leather along seam line; pound flat with a heavy mallet. Apply an even coat of rubber cement to underside of seam allowances and corresponding areas on leather under seam allowances. Let rubber cement dry for one minute before you press these down. Then ease seam allowances down onto leather beneath, smoothing out bumps with your fingers. Use the cobbler's hammer to pound seam allowances firmly into place. If you work slowly and use even pressure, sides will be evenly flattened.

CRAFTNOTES

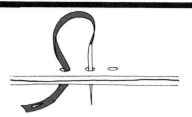

Sewing with Leather Lacing: Cut lacing 6 inches longer than seam. Make a small slit in one end. Thread other end. Bring needle up through first hole from wrong side; insert through second hole.

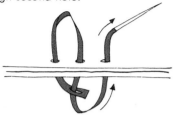

Put the needle through the slit at end of lace, and come up through the next hole.

Continue stitching through holes. Be sure lacing does not get twisted. Do not pull so tight that leather puckers.

To make the last stitch, pull needle down through last hole, or make one more hole so needle ends on the wrong side.

Secure this last stitch by slipping the needle under the previous stitches made on the underside of the seam.

When you pull lacing through last stitch, tug to lock it in. Cut off excess, leaving a tail to prevent its slipping back.

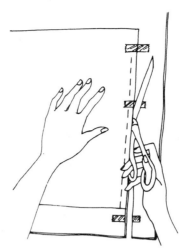

Cutting leather to patterns: The easiest way to cut leather accurately is to follow a cardboard pattern, held in place with masking or cellophane tape. Simply tape cardboard to leather so it is secure. Then, with sharp shears, cut along edge of cardboard pattern, cutting through the tape as you go. Use your free hand to keep the pattern in the right position on the leather as you continue cutting. Never pin patterns to leather.

Holding seams for sewing: To hold two matching edges of leather firmly together while you sew, use rubber cement, or hold them with masking tape placed at 1½-inch intervals. Stitch over tape; remove it later.

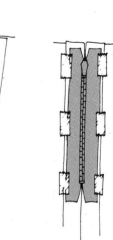

Sewing a zipper onto leather: Fold back the seam allowances for the zipper opening, and brush the undersides and the surface just beneath with rubber cement, as shown in the sketch at left. When the rubber cement has dried, in about 60 seconds, press the cement-covered surfaces together, and hammer them flat. Fasten the zipper in place face down with tapes as shown in sketch at right. Stitch zipper into place, then remove tapes.

Say It with a Smile

Ray Gill has made a career of cartooning since he was 17. He developed the forerunner of the storyboard technique used in movies and television, worked with Paul Terry, wrote the first Mighty Mouse comic books and, later, the comic-book version of Bob Montana's Archie. Artist, writer, and editor, he is best known in the fine-arts world of found-object sculpture for his three-dimensional "cartoon" pieces, which can be seen at the Wantagh N.Y., Public Library.

Cartoonist Ray Gill, on these two pages interprets cartooning history, from cave art, below, and political cartoons, opposite page, to the comics which are depicted as Gill's own style across the bottom of these two pages.

Cartooning is telling stories in pictures. Its earliest beginnings were the cave drawings of prehistoric man. Primitive societies used picture stories as a method of communication, as well as a magic performed to bring good fortune. About 20,000 B.C. Cro-Magnon man made colored cave drawings similar to the drawings below.

Each era, Egyptian, Greek, medieval, Renaissance, produced its own art, always with the same storytelling quality. Line drawing, so much like today's

Cave drawings, represented here, are among the earliest records of story-telling pictures.

Drawings that satirized politics eventually led to single-panel and strip cartoons—"Born 30 Years Too Soon" and "The Timid Soul," for instance—all peopled by figures everyone could laugh at and identify with.

402

cartoons, was etched, painted, carved, and lithographed.

The word cartoon was first applied to the full-size design or sketch for
an oil painting, tapestry, or mosaic. The word acquired its present meaning
by accident. In 1841, when both the Palace of Westminster (where the British
Houses of Parliament convene) and the British comic weekly *Punch* were in
their beginnings, Prince Albert commissioned designs for frescoes to adorn
the walls of the new palace. Some of them were so bad that *Punch* reproduced
the cartoons for the designs and captioned them satirically. The *Punch*
cartoon was born, and the word acquired its new meaning.

Caricature and satire combined with line drawing grew to be a powerful
weapon, socially and politically. The political cartoon has long been
recognized as a force to be respected. Editorials may or may not be read and
understood, but almost everyone understands cartoons, and they have brought
about both social and political change.

Publications such as *The New Yorker* and the old *Life* popularized single-
panel cartoons with one-line captions. Sometimes not even the one line was
needed. Earlier, the comic strip was created. The "Yellow Kid," by Richard F.
Outcault, so called because it was imprinted with yellow, was first
published by the New York *World*. It was recognized as a winner by William
Randolph Hearst, who enticed Outcault to his New York *Journal*. The *World*
brought him back. In the ensuing controversy, the term yellow journalism was
born, and so were colored comics. Syndication of comic strips led to their
appearance in papers around the world. Then came the comic magazine.

Sketches satirizing political figures, such as this take-off on drawings typical of the British
comic weekly, *Punch*, were the forerunners of modern comic strips.

Heroes of strip cartooning, like "Dagwood Bumstead," shown in Ray Gill's interpretation,
proliferated and evolved into superheroes such as the "Flash Gordon" type. More
recently anti-heroes, such as "Mr. Natural" and "Fritz the Cat" rival Flash Gordon
in popularity.

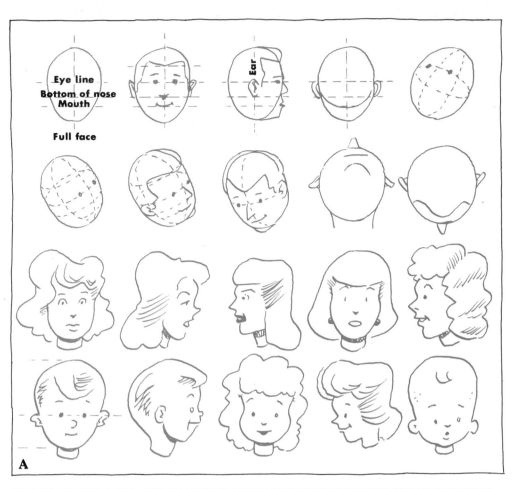

Figure A: Sketches at the right illustrate the basic oval used in cartooning to represent the human head and show how the angle of the oval, and lines added to the oval, can create cartoon representations of the faces of men, women, and children. These simplified faces acquire depth and life by the addition of pencil shading in the three sketches above. Working with a blown-out eggshell supported by an eggcup, you can develop a feeling for the shape the oval assumes from various angles. Dashed lines show how relative positions of features remain unchanged even when angle at which the head is seen does change. Hairline is added after the features have been positioned and does much, as you can see in figures A and B, to characterize the person as man, older man, woman, child.

Graphic Arts
Heads, faces, expressions

Acquiring a cartooning technique and using it with kindness can add more to daily family and community life than you might suppose. A cartoon congratulating a child on a scholastic feat or a sports success means more to him than would a simple verbal O.K. A cartoon view of a family problem or chore to come can express it without sting. You can also use cartooning techniques to dramatize community messages and advertise community projects.

Don't be put off by the notion that you don't have artistic talent. Cartoons can be put together in a fairly mechanistic way, once you know how.

Choose a Style That Suits You
There are many kinds of cartoons to experiment with, and one of these will probably seem easier than others. The simplest is the single-panel cartoon (see pages 408 and 409), whose function is to illustrate a joke, which may or may not be expressed with a gag line below. Once you have learned how to make a single-panel-cartoon character, you can trace and cut out your character, pin his arms, legs, and head together with pushpins, affix him to your drawing paper, and trace him in the various actions needed to illustrate a panel or even a panel series.

Or you can scribble a doodle, like those on pages 412 and 413, and from the basic forms evolved create characters that illustrate a single-panel cartoon or a strip or a story.

Since all cartoons start with one or more main characters, drawing these characters is the first technique to acquire. The head and facial expression are the most important elements in these figures.

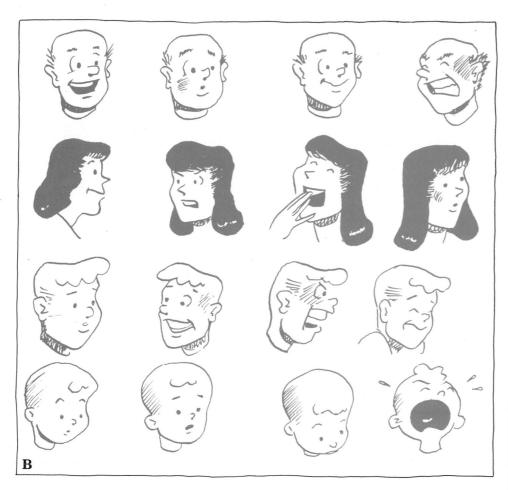

B

Figure B: Sketches above and at the left show vivid facial expressions created by pencil lines on the basic oval faces illustrated on the opposite page. By studying the drawings, you can see how simply you can portray emotions. A good technique for mastering the drawing of facial expressions is to look in a mirror and make faces at yourself—really let yourself go. Exaggerate your features for comic effect. Study the faces of your friends, and try to discover mannerisms and characteristics that you can turn to good comic use. Remember that, to an aspiring cartoonist, the whole world is a classroom.

For drawing purposes, the human head is egg shaped, as in figure A. Fullface, eye line is about halfway between head top and chin. Hair is not included in relative placement of features. Bottom of the nose is halfway between eye line and bottom of the chin, mouth about halfway between nose and chin. A child's eye line is lower than an adult's; but nose and mouth distances are the same. The lower the eye line, the younger the child. These measurements are simplified but practical. Try them, and adjust them to suit yourself. For a profile, the ear is drawn in the center. Its top is even with the eye line; its bottom lines up with bottom of the nose.

Start with Eggshell Models
To get started on drawing heads, make some models. Empty and clean three eggs. Pierce each end with a large darning needle, and stir the contents. Take a deep breath, and blow the egg out of the shell. Turn one egg large end down for a man, two eggs small end down for a woman and a child. Place the eggs in eggcups so they will stand upright. With a felt marker, draw dotted lines to locate features, as in figure A. Turn the eggs so the faces look up, down, or to the side. Continue to use these models to sketch from until you feel you are proficient enough to work without them.

Before trying to draw an expression, feel the emotion yourself. The cartoonist is writer, director, cameraman, and actor. See the sketches above for simple ways to indicate feelings. Curve the mouth up for a smile, down for anger. Look in a mirror and make your face show the feeling you want to portray. Then draw it.

You will discover that you have natural acting ability and that your expressions can be interpreted in terms of lines. Your drawing style will be personal. Start with ordinary paper and a soft pencil. Then graduate to a medium-size black felt pen and Bristol board.

Figure C: This simple mannequin, made of corks and pipe cleaners, with modeling clay for a base, will be a big help when you are learning to draw the human figure. Bend it into different positions, and sketch it from several angles.

C

▶ Figure D: Two paper cut-out puppets are useful aids. One represents a boy, and the other, almost identical but smaller, a girl. Trace them, cut them out of cardboard, pin them in poses, as shown, and draw from them.

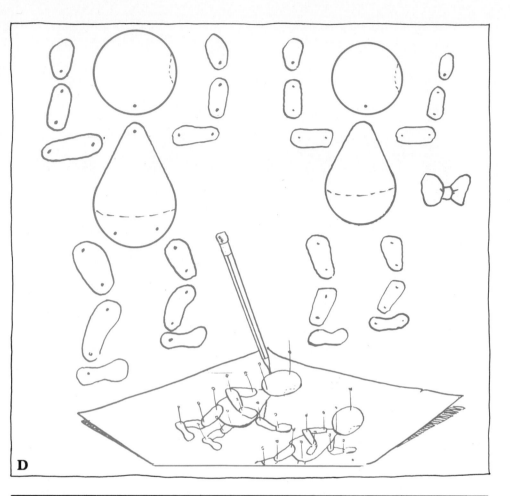

D

Graphic Arts
Drawing figures and hands

The best way to learn how to draw the human figure is by sketching from life. There are other ways, and two are illustrated in figures C and D.

If you have, or can buy, an artist's mannequin, a figure with moveable limbs, you can pose it in any action and sketch from it. You can make a simplified version of an artist's mannequin as shown in figure C. Use different sizes of corks for head, chest, and hips, and connect them with sections of thick pipe cleaners. Pipe cleaners make the arms and legs. A lump of modeling clay serves as a base. Extensions from bottoms of the heels stuck into the clay hold the figure upright. Bend the pipe-cleaner limbs and spine to achieve any pose you want.

Or trace the disjointed figures in figure D; transfer them to cardboard, and cut them out. Tape down the corners of the board you are going to draw on, so it won't move about. Lay the figures (one is for a small boy, one for a small girl) on the board; position them for the action, and pin to the board. Pin the pieces together with common straight pins, one at each joint plus any needed to hold the figures in place. Trace around the figures in pencil, and then remove them.

I developed these figures into characters for a daily single-panel cartoon called "Adam 'n Evie." Samples of this feature are shown on pages 408 and 409. Study them, and use them as a reference.

Balance is the key to making an action look right. If the top of the figure bends forward, the middle must bend backward for balance. If the figure is walking, moving ahead, it must lean forward a bit. Action is achieved by drawing in balance. Study other cartoons to learn how they were done.

E

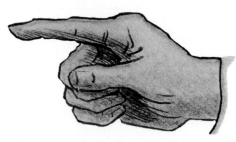

Figure E: Sketches at left show how the hands of men, women, and children differ. Look at the second row in the figure. A man's hands tend to be massive and powerful. The fingers of a woman's hands, third row, are slender and tapering. The hands of a child have a soft, chubby look, as in the fourth row. Hands can be extremely effective in conveying expression. Pose and observe your own hands, and draw from them. Also, keep an eye on other people's hands, and watch how they hold and move them. Hand above, indicating direction, suggests one way hands can be used in cartoons to "talk."

How To Draw Hands

Hands are the hardest part of the body to draw in cartooning. Treat them mechanically at first. Simplify them. Or have your cartoon characters wear mittens, if you find this necessary.

Eventually, however, most cartoonists face the fact that a hand has four fingers and a thumb, and they draw them. So that you will make the hands in proper proportion to the figure, remember that an open hand is about the size of a face and that palm breadth is about the same as the distance from bottom of nose to tip of chin. It is also helpful to think of a hand as a square block. Get the block in perspective, and the fingers and thumb will fit on nicely. If you go at it as if the hand were an octopus, that is exactly what it will look like when you draw it.

Learn from Your Own Hands

Pose one hand doing an action, and draw what you see. Then copy the hands in figure E. Correct what you have drawn. The result should be pretty good.

Women's hands are more graceful and slender than most men's hands. The **little finger juts out; the thumb is held close to the palm; the hand may** hang limply from the wrist. Draw these hands with a smooth line rather than an angular line.

Children's hands are smaller, fingers and thumb shorter and pudgier. Like women's hands, they are graceful, however, and display similar elements, such as extended little fingers and tentative gentleness—think of a child's hands holding a butterfly. Again, sketch from life whenever possible. A trick: Draw the main action line of a child's hands quickly; then add the rest. This technique is also good for sketching animals. Children and animals move too fast for a studied portrait. Finally, realize that hands usually play a big part in conveying expression. Try to capture this function.

Graphic Arts
Single-panel cartoons

Heads, faces, expressions, figures are the basic elements in the simplest of all cartoons, the single-panel gag. The other elements are the accessories that surround the main figures, the background or setting, and the gag line.

By accessories to the main figures, I mean the pirate ship, for instance, in the cartoon at left and the naive toys held by Adam and Evie. The pirate ship sets the reader up—prepares him—for the gag line. The toys emphasize the innocence of the children and counterpoint their would-be-mature interpretations of the world.

Use Adam and Evie to evolve single-panel cartoons of your own. The basic shapes that compose the youngsters are two circles, one for the head, one for the hips, and a cone shape for the chest area. Using circles and cone shapes, you can create other accessories and characters as needed: toys, adults, or, perhaps, a big dog, which can pull Adam on his wagon, lick his face, eat his ice-cream cone.

The setting for your cartoons will require drawing some form of background. The easiest background is a natural, slightly curved, horizon line, with a bit of foliage for decoration, as in the cowboy cartoon, left. A few simple lines can indicate a fence and sidewalk, as in the cartoon on the opposite page. But to draw background properly, you must understand a bit about drawing in perspective. To simplify this, think about looking down a railroad track, and remember how the rails seem to come together when they reach the horizon. This is called the vanishing point. This visual principle makes objects appear smaller in the distance. Dark objects appear to be lighter. To use this principle in cartooning, study figure F, and note how all the lines in this one-point-perspective drawing converge. I used Evie's eye line to determine the point of convergence. I stuck a pin in the board at this point, placed a

"I guess they had pirates so they'd have something to think about on those long, dull voyages."

"Say, do they call this a revolver because they start revolutions with it?"

"I can't figure out some people. They keep saying to me, 'Isn't he wonderful for his age.' But they say the same thing about Grandpa, and he's an awful lot older than me."

ruler against the bottom of the pin and across the drawing, and drew the dashed line. This gave me the perspective for the face and the sidewalk. The two fence lines and the single sidewalk line were drawn to reach the same vanishing, or horizon, point. If a second sidewalk line were drawn, it should touch the same point. Using two points, two pins, one on each side of the cartoon, you can draw two-point perspective. The horizon eye line is your position. For a top view, raise the eye line, and draw down from it. For a low horizon, looking up, place your eye line low, and draw the perspective lines down from it.

Try drawing a water glass. Hold it above your eye line, and you can see the bottom to draw it. With the glass even with your eyes, top and bottom circles seem like straight lines. Hold it low, and you can see the top.

F

Figure F: This "Adam 'n Evie" cartoon illustrates one-point-perspective drawing. Dashed line from Evie's eye to horizon point is used as a guide to determine the vanishing point, at which all horizontal lines converge, as shown here, and individual objects vanish.

You can approach gag writing in one of two ways. Write a funny line first, and then draw the characters in suitable poses. Or draw the characters in an interesting situation, and write the line afterward.

The theme of "Adam 'n Evie" is that he is always doing the talking, explaining to her how the world really is. The fact that some of his explanations bear no relation to the truth is irrelevant—he has interpreted things to his own satisfaction, and this is all that matters to him.

Gag Lines To Illustrate

Try illustrating this line: "The world is like a big beach ball, Evie—only all the water is on the inside." Another: "I used to think dogs were boy animals and cats were girl animals. Now I'm not so sure." Another: "Sure it's a happy picture of me. My father said if I didn't smile, he'd kill me."

"Guess what the Japanese have come up with now —FANS! No motors, no batteries, no nothing! You just hold them in your hand and wave them!" 409

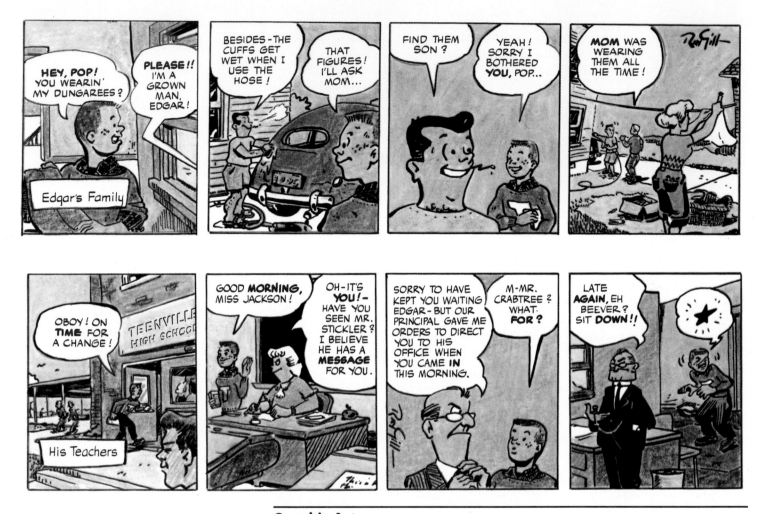

Graphic Arts
Drawing a comic strip

The comic strips shown above were for a teen-age character named Edgar Beever. First, the dialogue was written. Then balloons and lettering were drawn; after that, characters and backgrounds were drawn. Notice how the action, like camera angles, takes into consideration close-ups, long shots, angles of view, and even an amount of detail from panel to panel. The idea is to balance the strip. If the first drawing is a close shot with a simple background, the second panel can be farther away and have more detail. The third, for relief, has no background, and the fourth has plenty.

After the figures were roughed in with pencil, the hands, features, and details were inked in with black India ink and a fine-pointed flexible pen, which provides the greatest control. Clothing, objects, and backgrounds were inked in with a small No. 1 sable brush. Lettering and balloon outlines were inked in with a narrow, flat-nib pen, heavy lettering with a wider pen.

If a mistake is made, wait for the ink to dry; then scratch off unwanted ink with a single-edge razor blade. Erase carefully; then paint over the scratched-off area with Chinese white, using another small sable brush.

Always clean your brushes and pens when you have finished using them. If brushes dry with ink or paint on them, they become stiff and bristles break off. If pens are not kept clean, they clog.

In creating a comic strip, list your characters, exactly who they are and what their characteristics will be. This is not unlike writing a play. You should balance everything, even characters. Keeping their personalities consistent is difficult, but only at first.

Comic Strips without Words

Below are two examples of a comic strip without words. The action pictured in the panels carries the message. This is a particularly effective approach for children who cannot read. And it is comprehensible no matter what one's language. It is a throwback, in fact, to the early story drawings of primitive art.

The main ingredients in a comic strip without words, aside from the character or characters, are the locale of the action and the props it provides. What the character does with the props is what conveys the story. Some of the best liked and most famous comic strips have been those that did not rely on words to get their meaning across.

I call the little character pictured here Tinker, because he loves to make things, to utilize objects in an imaginative way, and can always think his way out of impossible situations through a kind of improvised logic. It doesn't matter to him if his plotted fantasy doesn't work; the fantasy that develops instead is just as pleasing—or frightening.

The way to get ideas for cartoons is to become a people watcher or, in this case, a child watcher. Youngsters do some of the most wonderful and some of the dumbest things imaginable. Always, however, their unfettered imaginations are working for them. They sit in an old-tire swing and they are in the basket of a huge balloon, drifting skyward. Tinker paints a pussycat with tiger stripes, below, and when it turns on him, it becomes a tiger. Washing off the stripes eliminates the threat.

Once you get the pattern, however, your own childhood imagination will flower again, and you can go real children one better. They are not always cute or funny or ingenious. But the children in your imaginary world can be, because you make them so, and that is a great way of staying young.

These comic strips without words have only one character, Tinker. No words are needed to explain how he reacts to situations.

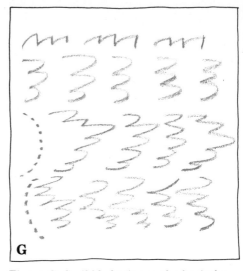

Figure G: Scribbled m's are the basis for impromptu cartoons. Do them vertically, linked continuously in curves, as shown by dotted lines.

Graphic Arts
Self-starter cartoons

Blank paper is a threat all artists and writers must cope with. I have invented a way to eliminate it. The beginnings for cartoon faces in figure G were drawn by quickly scribbling m's sideways until they accidentally began to take on the features of cartoon characters. This is easy, although it does take a bit of practice. When you get the hang of it, you can scribble a couple of m's, and you are off and running. The phenomenon is that, once you have drawn the characters, your subconscious mind usually can supply funny lines for them to say.

In figure G, a series of script m's is written across the top. The second row shows the m's scribbled sideways like extended 3s. The next row shows the m's with added bumps, five or six this time, and extended to the right (note dotted line) to form something like a face. This would be the male face. The m's in the bottom row follow the convex dotted-line pattern, for the female face. The pointed bottoms of the m's provide sharper features.

In approximately the center of a piece of paper, draw some extended m's as shown at left in figure H. Learn to make erratic bumps in the m's, so the features are somewhat different each time. The second sketch shows placement of the eyes, which is very important—now the face takes shape. The next sketch (remember that a head is egg shaped) shows the finished heads, with hairdos. Then, as in the fourth sketch, clothes and accessories are added.

Scribble . . .   **. . . add eyes . . .**   **. . . hair . . .**   **. . . clothes, and it's almost finished.**

Figure H: The apparently random scribbles at left, above, resolve into the finished cartoon below.

Figure I: Adding the background completes the drawing of the cartoon. All that remains is to think up a gag line such as the one in the text, or you can reverse the process and think up your joke first.

Background details complete the picture (figure I). Now comes the magic: the funny line. Funny or not, you will have a good idea of what the man is saying. The reason? I believe your subconscious mind is funnier than your conscious mind. The line that came to me was: "I don't think my mother would believe I've taken up pipe smoking; she only lets me smoke cigars."

On the opposite page are three more cartoons developed from scribbled m's.

Cartoons as Communication
One great value of cartooning is that it can communicate information in an amusing way. During World War II, for instance, cartoons instructed people in safety procedures and warned them against divulging secrets that might be useful to the enemy. Robert Osborne's famous cartoon character, Dilbert, an aviation cadet who made ridiculous errors in judgment, was used by the United States Navy to teach fledgling pilots safe flying procedures. The lessons were both funny and unforgettable.

Once you have developed a cartooning technique, you will find many uses for it. You can make a cartoon collage to attract youngsters' attention and pound home some points. Any sign from "Brush Your Teeth" to "Put Out the Garbage!" can become a friendly reminder rather than nagging if it is emphasized by a simple cartoon drawing.

"And you can tell your publisher I'm stopping the paper because I don't cotton to your editorial policies!"

"Oh, sure, I know your pipe drives the mosquitoes away, but I'm driving fifty miles an hour!"

Cartooning in Schools
Every teacher, I think, should have to pass a test in cartooning. Bulletin boards with cartoons not only attract attention but make people feel better. Playful lampooning between teacher and student is healthy if done with cartoons. The school paper should always include some cartoons. Special announcements are less liable to be thrown away if they are enlivened by humorous or interesting cartoons.

Cartooning in the Office
Cartoons, with their joshing quality, are a good way for management or staff to make points, and they help keep morale high. Who is in the doghouse? A cartoon is the kindest way to tell. Who is king of the salesmen? A sketch of a man resembling the salesman and wearing a crown is a royal tribute. He will probably take it home and frame it.

Cartooning for Community Projects
Because cartoons tell their message so easily, they have long been used in advertising. Borrow from ad agencies' bag of tricks and use cartoons to make your point in community activities. Keep Our Town Clean committees in many communities have used cartoons to convey their message. P.T.A. meetings, grass-roots political campaigns, garage sales, and many other projects can be announced effectively by cartoons made by an interested amateur.

To make multiple copies, see the Craftnotes in the article "Greeting Cards," which explains how to prepare art for reproduction by a printer. Use an office duplicating machine if only a few dozen copies are needed.

Cartoons in Decorating
Cartoon animals delight children and make good themes for children's rooms. They can be sketched small and enlarged for wall decorations by using the grid system described on page 57 of Volume One. Or sketch them from shadows projected by a magic lantern or with the camera-obscura method illustrated in the entry "Cameras." Bold color effects can be added with paint or patterned, self-adhesive plastic. This material comes in feltlike fabric in black, red, green, and gold.

You can use cartoons on furniture or screens, as wall hangings, as designs for needlework rugs or pillows. Draw them in ink, paint them, or make them in almost any medium, even painted glass with a crinkled-foil background.

For related projects, see the entries "Calligraphy," "Photography," "Silhouettes," and "Valentines."

"Then they called me in! 'Horace,' they said, 'if there's one man here who would know exactly what Tarzan would do in a case like this — it's YOU!'"

413

CARVING
Soap to Vegetables

Creative carving is the cutting away of material to produce a form or to decorate a surface. To a Michelangelo, this meant freeing a statue from the marble in which it was imprisoned. But lesser mortals working with more amenable materials must still have a feel for the material they plan to work with before they start to carve. Each substance has particular qualities of hardness, softness,and brittleness. Each has a different degree of responsiveness to cutting and shaping.

The easiest way for the beginner to learn about materials is to experiment with them. Explore them with your fingers and fingernails. Break off a portion of the material and examine the result. This will tell you how brittle the material is, and whether the break is irregular, or relatively clean and straight. Next, with a knife, find out how the material reacts to shallow and deep cutting, and to making intricate shapes which might crumble or collapse if the wrong material were used. As an example, the experienced soap carver knows better than to carve a figure with spindly legs that might collapse.

Soap and paraffin are, however, good materials for the beginner to work with while he is learning basic carving techniques. They are relatively soft, and can be carved into three-dimensional shapes without encountering the problems of harder-to-work materials such as stone or wood. Soap and paraffin are also more forgiving of mistakes, and permit repairs it would be difficult to make in harder materials. Their softness also permits experimentation with rough, smooth, or textured finishes. In addition, such soft carvings are inexpensive, require very few special tools, and, as is shown in the projects that follow, make attractive gifts.

Another form of soft carving deals with the shaping of fresh fruits and vegetables, such as those shown in the projects beginning on page 418. Although they are far more perishable than objects carved of soap or paraffin, vegetables do provide the beginning carver with a variety of interesting substances with which to experiment. And, as so many carvers have found, much of the enjoyment of carving lies in the experimenting.

In addition to being a sculptor in soft materials and a painter, Jo-Anne Jarrin is one of The Family Creative Workshop's *art editors. Her extensive background in the arts includes work with art galleries, appraisers, publishers, and a graphic-design firm. In spare moments, she tends an indoor garden of avocados.*

Carving and Molding
Making fish from soap

Carving soap is not as easy as it might seem. As with any form of carving, the key to success is practice and a working knowledge of the medium. There are two main categories of soap. One is the firm, Castile variety; the other is softer and tends to crumble easily. Both varieties can be used successfully once you have become accustomed to working with them. Bear in mind that you will need a little practice and that any failures, as well as the chipped-away crumbs, can be saved and used for washing up.

Unwrap the soap, and let it stand about 24 hours in a dry place so excess moisture in the bar will evaporate. Do this with several cakes so alternates will be available when you get down to work. A simple project to start with is the fish on page 416. Or sketch an original design on a sheet of paper. The simpler the design, the fewer the carving problems, especially for the beginner. Avoid too many angles or curves until you become more expert. Gather together a dull paring knife (a dull edge is easier to control), a felt marker, and a pie plate or tray to work on.

Punch-bowl pumpkin at top, pompon radishes and rosebuds, turnip pompon, celery stalk sections, carrot and cucumber pinwheels, scallion brushes, tomato rose. (Directions on pages 418 to 421.)

Gently remove any markings from the soap, as shown in photograph 1. Then, if you are making the fish, mark the main cutting areas, as in figure A. When lines have been drawn, follow the directions with photographs 2, 3, 4, and 5 for carving. It is important that the main cuts, such as cutting away the semicircles, be made evenly from front to back of the cake of soap. Never cut away a large area all at once. Unless you cut away gradually, you will risk breakage. Several shallow scoopings produce much less stress on the soap than a large gouge would. Also, shallow cuts are easier to control than deep ones. If a fairly large portion does break off, it can be reattached by moistening along the break and holding the piece in place until dry. After you have shaped an area, smooth it with your fingers and facial tissue.

1: Hold the knife with the blade almost parallel to the bar of soap. Trying not to cut deeply, shave off or shave out the brand name and any raised edges.

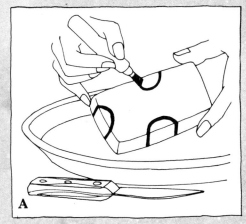

A

Figure A: Using a felt marker, draw three semicircles on the soap. Continue the lines down the sides, as shown. Do not press with marker, or ink flow will stop.

2: Cut into the bar of soap until you have removed the entire semicircle, from front to back. Work carefully, with gentle strokes, to prevent breakage.

3: To finish shaping the fish, carve head outlines, remove all sharp edges and round off corners. Make shallow, glancing strokes. Work the entire shape at once.

Fish are carved in rainbow colors from bars of soap, with the aid of your paring knife and nimble fingers.

4: Insert the knife point into one side of the head. Carefully twirl the knife to make a circular hole for the fish's eye. Repeat on the other side of the head.

5: Holding the head firmly, ease knife blade ½ inch into the soap. Just above this cut and angled down to meet it, make a second cut to complete the fish's mouth.

Carving and Molding
Relief design in wax

$ ▨ 🧍 ⚗

Of the many waxes available, paraffin is the best for carving. You can buy it in small cakes at grocery stores or in larger, more economical slabs at art-supply shops. To carve a cake or slab in relief, as I did the fruit-bowl scene below, first trace your design on the wax with a toothpick. Then, using an angular gouge (figure B), cut along the lines that will be the deepest parts of the design. Next, use a curved gouge to shape the curved elements in the design, taking only small shavings with each cut until you have the shape you want. For small details, such as the grapes, try moving your hand closer to the tip of the gouge, as you would a pencil, for better control. Use a flat carving tool to shave away the larger background areas. Deepen the original cuts with an angular gouge if you find you don't have enough depth. Sweep away wax crumbs that accumulate as you work with a soft bristle brush. Finish by gently rubbing highest areas with your fingers and facial tissue. This will give the carving a translucent sheen.

To carve an object in the round from a paraffin block, melt wax in the top of a double boiler, pour into a half-gallon milk carton, and place in cold water until wax hardens. Peel off milk carton, sketch object's outline on the block, as you did the fish, page 416, and you are ready to carve.

6: A good way to guide the tool is to place your free hand over its shaft as you move it slowly from behind. In this manner, you can maintain better control over the length and depth of cuts.

7: An alternate method is to place your free hand under the hand moving the tool. This will prevent overcutting. Never rest your free hand ahead of the tool; if you do you will risk a nasty gouge.

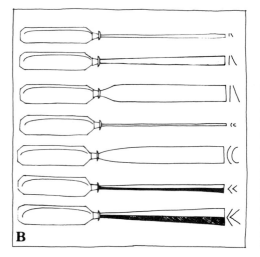

Figure B: A set of wax-carving tools. The top three are flat and are used to cut away large areas smoothly, as well as to produce well-defined outlines in the wax. Below these are two curved gouging tools, for scooping out curved portions. The last two are angular gouges, used to deepen outlines and details for better definition. A typical cut is shown at the right of each tool. It is not essential to have all of them, but at least one of each variety is recommended for successful wax carving. These sturdy and versatile tools can also be used to carve linoleum and wood blocks. They are not expensive and are available at art-supply and hobby shops.

8: The secret of making relief carvings such as this fruit bowl scene is to work slowly with small cuts or shavings, until you have obtained the shape you want.

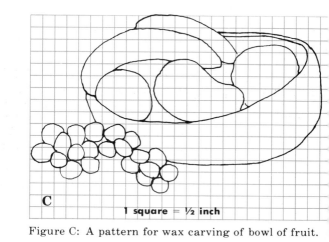

1 square = ½ inch

Figure C: A pattern for wax carving of bowl of fruit.

Carving vegetables, fruits ¢ ⊠ 👪 🎇

Vegetable and fruit carving is said to have had its beginnings in the Far East, where the presentation of food played a significant role in its preparation and suitability for consumption. Because of religious beliefs concerning harmony and balance, food was supposed to appeal to all the senses, not only to the sense of taste. Following along these lines in the West, Antonin Careme, a master chef of the early nineteenth century, proposed the fundamental rule that the decoration should gracefully enhance and not overpower the dish. Decoration to stimulate the appetite can take a variety of forms, ranging from the artful placement of a sprig of fresh parsley to elaborate sculptural forms, from garnishing to creating delightful edible centerpieces. With a sharp knife, fresh fruits and vegetables, and some pre-party spare time, you can achieve impressive results.

Large, hard-skinned melons are ideal for carving and may be the focal point of a centerpiece. A watermelon can be formed into a serving bowl and filled with scooped-out melon balls. A Casaba or winter melon, carved on the outside

Carve the vegetables well in advance of your party or special meal, so you can give proper attention to shaping them. Placed in a bowl of ice water and stored in the refrigerator, they will keep for days.

Skin is removed from rind of this pumpkin in a floral pattern to make a festive container for sweet cider or soup.

9: With a dark grease pencil, outline your design on the pumpkin. Repeat the motif around the circumference, making sure to work within the boundary lines.

10: Use a curved gouge (see figure B, page 417) to cut carefully along your outlines (see also the photograph on page 414). Watch out for your fingers.

to simulate an oriental vase and then hollowed out, can function as a tureen for soup made from its flesh. A carved pumpkin can hold cold soup, cider or pudding for an autumn luncheon. It won't flavor the contents. The only restriction is the melon's seasonal availability.

In working with a pumpkin, there are several considerations to note. If you plan to fill it with food or drink, you must carefully remove the top with a sharp knife and scoop out all except the firm outer flesh. (The seeds may be kept and baked for an appetizing snack.) In this case, you cannot keep

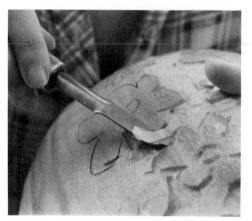

11: With a flat tool, gently remove the skin outside each flower and in its center. No need to cut deeply: With the tool, simply lift off the skin in these areas.

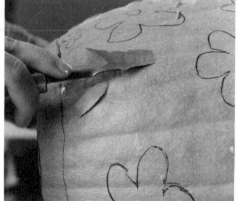

12: In large open areas between the flowers, make long strokes with a flat carving tool to remove big pieces of skin, but keep clear of outlined areas.

the scooped-out pumpkin for more than three days, because it would become soft and sag. If you wish to use the pumpkin repeatedly in centerpieces, leave it intact. Several coats of shellac applied to the carved pumpkin will enable you to keep it for an entire season.

When you are cutting the design into the pumpkin skin, use towels to soak up the beads of moisture that will be released. If you wish, wear rubber gloves to avoid getting this sticky substance on your hands. Draw boundary lines around the circumference approximately 1 ½ inches below the top and above the base of the pumpkin. The floral patterns you cut should not extend into these 1 ½ inch spaces, so the pumpkin can be handled without damage to the incised design. After you have carved the pumpkin, refrigerate it until party time.

13: To make a turnip pompon, place pared turnip between two wooden chopsticks on a cutting board. With sharp knife, slice thinly down to sticks, making parallel cuts.

14: Turn turnip, and cut across first slices at right angles, down to the sticks. When all cuts are made, place turnip in ice water. Petals of the pompon will open.

15: To make a radish rosebud, trim off the root tip. With the point of a sharp knife, cut petal shapes in the radish from the top to just above the base. Then slice down until each petal is freed.

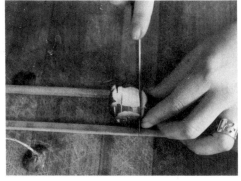

16: To make a radish pompon, place radish between two chopsticks, and cut crossed slices as you did the turnip. Then drop into ice water. Oblong radishes work best.

17: When you place a carved vegetable in water, check the temperature. If the water becomes warm, add several ice cubes. The water must always be ice-cold.

Carving small vegetables into floral forms, like those pictured in color on page 414, requires a sharp knife and patience. A nearby bowl of ice water provides the magic to open vegetable flowers and crisp decorative accents such as carrot curls. Always prepare several more of each design than you will need, so that when you are arranging them in your centerpiece or as garnishes, you can select the best. The more you carve the more you will learn about the possibilities of particular fruits and vegetables. Working with turnips, for instance, might give you ideas about potatoes. The carvings described here are, for the most part, traditional floral forms.

18: Clean and scrape a thick carrot. With a sharp knife, make V-shape lengthwise grooves, evenly spaced, around the carrot. The grooves should be ⅛ inch deep.

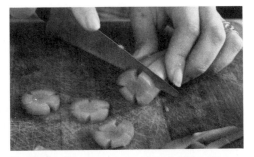

19: When all grooves are cut, gently slice the carrot pinwheels. Each slice should be about ⅛ inch thick. Cucumber pinwheels are made the same way.

20: U-shape slices of celery are made with quick strokes of a knife held at an angle. Try to make slices wafer-thin.

21: Trim bulb and upper stalks from a scallion. Make four cuts, 1 inch long, in each end. Immerse in ice water at once.

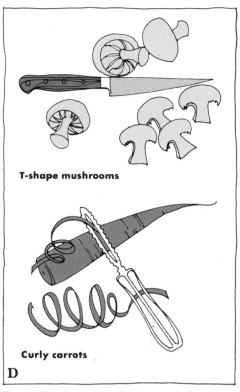

T-shape mushrooms

Curly carrots

D

Figure D: Above, top, T-shape mushrooms are made by cutting thin slices from stem to cap. A drop of lemon juice stops discoloration. Above, coil carrot parings and pin with toothpick. Place in ice water. A gay garnish, they are nice in salads.

But they should provide an inspiration for other designs. The Chinese, for example, carve the upper portions of extra-large carrots into miniature Buddhas. Before you know it, you will start looking at vegetables in the market with new eyes, alert to their carving and decorating potential.

The arrangement of your carved pieces is almost as important as the proper cutting. A primary rule is always to place your transformed vegetables and fruits on an undecorated platter or tray. Obviously, plates with colored patterns would compete and divert attention from your work. If you don't have a solid-color platter or tray, place a doily on a patterned one. A second rule is to avoid cluttering a platter. Several well-arranged plates will be far more attractive. If you want a more fanciful arrangement, try attaching your carved flowers with toothpicks, colored with green food coloring, to whole vegetables, such as a head of iceberg lettuce or stalks of celery. Or combine your carved pieces with real flowers. Let your imagination run wild and your radishes turn in to roses.

For information on related projects and crafts, see "Block Printing," "Foam," "Masks," "Puppets," "Scrimshaw," "Totem Poles," "Toys," "Whistles and Flutes."

22: Tomato roses are made from ripe, firm tomatoes. Beginning at one end, peel off, trying not to cut too deeply into the pulp.

23: Shape tomato-skin strip into a rose. Pin with a toothpick. Place in ice water.

CASTING

Art of Repetition

Toni Polich is an artist, sculptress, and an expert on making molds for casting. Her husband, Dick, is equally expert as a metallurgist and founder. Together they own and operate the Tallix Foundry in Peekskill, N.Y., where they make castings for world-famous sculptors, for museums, and for home craftsmen.

The oldest known cast was probably made by a dinosaur. He stepped into clay, millions of years ago, and made a footprint. This cavity hardened and later was filled with fresh, liquid clay. When the liquid clay dried and solidified in the old cavity, it was a replica of the footprint. This prehistoric incident demonstrated three essentials of casting: the model (the foot), the mold (the old clay), and the cast (the new clay that solidified).

Later, man discovered that an object like a seashell, when pressed into clay, produced a cavity that had the negative shape of the seashell. Still later, he found that materials like hot wax and very hot metals would, as they cooled to a solid state, retain the shape of the cavity that contained them. It wasn't long before man applied these observations to duplicating solid objects that he treasured. He called this invention casting.

Man's earliest known casts were made with basically the same techniques that are employed today. A figure or object was modeled from a plastic material like clay or wax and allowed to harden. If clay, the hardened model was coated with some parting agent like tallow, then impressed into another chunk of fresh, moist clay. If wax, it was surrounded by liquid clay, with a drain-off channel left through the clay. In both cases, the clay molds were allowed to dry and become solid. The embedded wax figure was removed by heating the clay and allowing the molten wax to run out the channel provided, which explains why this method was called the lost-wax process. The cavities thus produced were negative duplicates of the original. The molds were then filled with metal heated to the molten state. When the metal cooled and became solid, it retained the precise shape of the model. Some fine examples of the detailed and delicate replicas it is possible to produce with this method are the tiny gold lost-wax castings made in the pre-Columbian era by the Mixtec Indians of Mexico.

The two casting projects that follow use the old techniques but substitute some new materials. In casting plaster, the mold used is of synthetic rubber and the cast is of plaster; both materials were unknown in their present form a hundred years ago. In casting metal, you will use plaster and tin, but still follow essentially the lost-wax process that the ancient Mixtecs employed. Each method will duplicate your sculpture with great fidelity, preserving all the freedom and expressiveness you have given it. Both methods also produce casts that are far more durable than original sculptures made of modeling clay. The primary advantage of casting in plaster is that the mold is not destroyed in making the casting; hence several copies can be made from it. The primary advantage of using metal is, of course, that the casting will be even more durable than one made of plaster.

For each of the projects that follow, you will use a casting plaster sold under a variety of names, such as plaster of Paris, dental plaster, pottery plaster, and molding plaster. Casting plaster hardens much more quickly than wall plaster, which should not be used for casting. If you plan to make several castings, you will find it more economical to buy 100 pounds of casting plaster from a large sculpture- or ceramics-supply outlet, rather than a smaller quantity from a retail craft shop. Check the yellow pages of your telephone directory for either type of source. But be warned that casting plaster doesn't keep well, so don't buy too much. You will need about 10 pounds for the plaster-casting project on pages 424 to 429, and 5 pounds for the metal-belt-buckle project on pages 430 to 433.

Liquid, flexible molding compound is poured around a sculpted clay model inside the plaster container. As the compound hardens, it forms a mold for the final plaster cast.

Sculpted head of modeling clay can be reproduced with all its subtle detail by making a casting of it in plaster.

Many sculptors like to work with modeling clay because it can be shaped easily. But it doesn't get very hard. So when work sculptured in modeling clay has been finished, it will frequently be cast in plaster to give it durability.

Carving and Molding
Casting a head in plaster $$ 🕐 👤 🔬

Making a cast in plaster of one of your prized figurines or some other piece of sculpture is relatively easy. And the plaster cast will be a far more durable sample of your work. To make a cast about the size of the head shown at left, you will need 10 pounds or so of casting plaster, about 5 pounds of modeling clay (from an art-supply store), and about 2 quarts of polysulphide flexible molding compound. Check the yellow pages of your telephone directory under the heading Plastics, Raw Materials, for companies that sell the molding compound. One firm that sells it in small quantities by mail is Smooth-On Corporation, 1000 Valley Road, Gillette, N.J. 07933. The two quarts cost about $14.

Other materials and equipment you will need are a plastic dishpan or bucket for mixing plaster; a disposable container for mixing the liquid molding compound; a few pieces of cheesecloth or burlap to reinforce the plaster; a spatula to shape the plaster; a hammer and chisel to separate the plaster mold holder; a couple of old paintbrushes; a replaceable-blade modeling knife or scalpel to cut apart the flexible mold; some 1½-inch-wide flexible scrap-aluminum strips that can be cut into six 4- to 8-inch lengths and used as separators between the mold halves; four or five C-clamps, or ¼-by-1-inch scrap metal that can be cut into 6- to 8-inch lengths and bent to form clamps) to hold the mold together; a plastic bag large enough to cover the model; about 8 ounces each of kerosene and petroleum jelly, which are used to keep materials from sticking together.

For finishing the cast, you will need a small can of brown shoe polish and half a pint of benzene for thinning it; a 1-pound can of paste wax; a small bottle of bronze powder; a pint of shellac.

Your first step in making the cast is to build a temporary plaster base for the clay model. The base should be a rough square, extending about 3 inches beyond the model on all sides. The volume of water you mix with 2 or 3 pounds of plaster to make the base should about equal the volume of plaster. Pour water into the mixing container first; then sift plaster through your fingers into the water. Continue sifting quickly until the plaster no longer sinks in the water, indicating that there is enough. Now let the mixture soak for two or three minutes, until the plaster islands become damp. Then stir briskly with your hands for a couple of minutes until no islands remain and the plaster has thickened slightly (photograph 1).

You have about 15 to 20 minutes to mix plaster and form the base before the plaster becomes too hard to use. So don't dawdle. When it has thickened slightly, put a glob of it on the work surface, and with the spatula roughly shape it into a square. If it runs, keep pushing it back until it starts to set. Add more plaster until the base is about an inch thick. Carefully set

1: Mix casting plaster to make a temporary base for the model. If your skin is sensitive, it might be wise to wear rubber gloves or use a spatula while mixing.

2: Cover the model with a plastic bag to protect it from damage while the clay spacing layer and the plaster mold holder are being formed around the model.

the clay model in the center of the base while the plaster is still soft, so the model will sit solidly when the plaster dries.

Protecting the Model
Give the model a coat of shellac to protect it; let dry. Using an old paintbrush, cover the model and the base with a coat of petroleum jelly, thinned half-and-half with kerosene. Heat this mixture in a double boiler until it is warm; then stir to make sure it is well blended. This coating will keep the materials to be added later from sticking to the model or its base. Cover the model (but not the base) with a plastic bag, as in photograph 2. This provides further protection against the temporary layer of modeling clay that you will fit around the model as the next step. This clay layer acts as a temporary spacer between the model and the plaster mold holder.

Next step is to roll out clay into slabs, ¼ inch or less in thickness. Carefully fit the slabs around the model, as in photograph 3. Do not press hard against the model; you might damage it. The purpose is to establish a smooth wall covering the model, with an outer surface that has no cracks or corners that might interlock with the plaster you will apply later.

Next, build a small ridge around the vertical perimeter of the clay

3: Slabs of modeling clay form a wall around the model. The plaster mold holder is built over this wall. Then the plaster is split and the clay removed, leaving a void for the poured-rubber mold.

4: A thickened ridge is formed around the perimeter of the clay lining. Thin strips of aluminum inserted into this ridge make the parting line for the plaster mold holder. Strips are later discarded.

5: A new batch of casting plaster is mixed and applied to the clay liner to form the mold holder. Cheesecloth or burlap scraps are layered into the plaster to help reinforce it.

covering the model, and form two clay horns at the top, as in photograph 4. These horns will provide the opening through which the flexible molding compound will later be poured. Insert the thin 4- to 8-inch-long aluminum strips into the center of the clay ridge, working all the way around the ridge and letting the strips stick out an inch or more. These strips form a divider that will later enable you to pry the plaster mold holder apart, into two halves.

Now coat the outside of the clay surface with the same mixture of kerosene and petroleum jelly that you used on the model and its base.

Making the Mold Holder
To make the plaster mold holder mix 8 pounds of plaster with water, following the procedure you used for mixing the plaster for the base. Apply a thin coat of wet plaster over the modeling clay. Reinforce wet plaster with a layer of burlap or cheesecloth: don't let cheesecloth cross the metal parting strips.

Apply another coat of plaster, more burlap, and more plaster, until the plaster is almost an inch thick, as shown in photograph 5. As you build up the plaster, form several flat areas on either side of the parting strips; these can be used later as clamping surfaces (see photograph 10, page 427).

6: After plaster has hardened, mold holder is separated along metal parting strips. Work around the strips, using an old chisel or putty knife and light hammer taps.

Let the plaster mold holder air-dry overnight. When the plaster has hardened, it can be split into halves with a hammer and chisel; work chisel in along the edges of the metal parting strips, as in photograph 6. Remove these strips. If any modeling clay is stuck in the mold holder, remove it, as in photograph 7. Also, remove clay from the model. Set aside all this clay. Scour the mold holder's inner surface with steel wool. Fill any pinholes in the plaster (caused by air bubbles) with modeling clay, and smooth down. Then lubricate the inside of the mold holder (photograph 8) with the same mixture of petroleum jelly and kerosene used earlier. This will keep the liquid molding compound from sticking to the mold holder. Drill two $1/16$- or $1/32$-inch holes for air vents near the bottom of the mold holder (see figure A).

When the mold holder is placed around the sculpted model, there is a cavity where the modeling clay had been (photograph 9). This cavity will be filled with the liquid compound that forms the actual mold you will later use for the casting. Clamp the two halves of the mold holder together around the model, and seal the cracks with modeling clay, as in photograph 10. For clamps, I used metal strips cut to 6- and 8-inch lengths, then bent into a U-shape and tapped over the opposing flat surfaces on the mold-holder sides. Large C-clamps would work as well. Or you could use clothesline, belts, or even very heavy rubber bands to hold the two parts together. The important thing is that the parts are held together tightly and securely.

Now use modeling clay to secure short sections of cardboard tubing in the pouring holes left by the clay horns, as shown in photograph 10. These cardboard extensions will help increase the pressure of the liquid molding compound you will pour, forcing it more tightly around the mold.

Pouring the liquid molding compound is the next step. You must mix enough to fill the cavity between the model and the mold holder in a single pour. You can judge the amount fairly accurately by the amount of modeling clay you used to create the original cavity and have set aside. Work this clay into the shape of the mixing container, and measure the depth. Then fill the container with molding compound to this depth, plus an inch or two. Stir in the hardening agent according to manufacturer's instructions.

Pour the liquid molding compound into the mold holder through one of the

7: When the mold holder is separated, remove the modeling clay from it and from the sculpted model. Smooth the inside of the holder with fine steel wool.

8: Lubricate the inside of the mold holder with petroleum jelly thinned with kerosene. This will keep poured flexible mold from sticking to the plaster.

9: Mold holder is placed around model, which also has been coated with thinned petroleum jelly to keep the flexible mold from sticking. Note void left by clay.

cardboard tubes, as in photograph 11 and figure A. The other tube will let trapped air escape. Pour compound back and forth between mold holder and container to make sure crevices are filled. Then pour both tubes to the top. Let a little liquid trickle out of the drilled air-vent holes at the bottom, to show air has been forced out; then close vent holes with clay. Use a funnel to pour from a large container into the small cardboard tube.
Funnel mouth should fit into the tube.

Set aside the mold holder for a day while the flexible molding compound

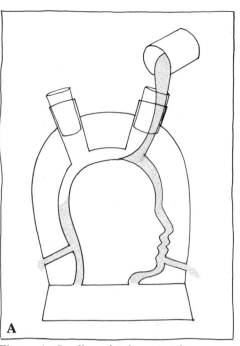

10: The plaster mold holder is clamped around the model. Cracks are sealed with modeling clay. One cardboard tube lets trapped air escape; one is for pouring in liquid compound, which forms the mold.

11: Liquid compound is poured into the mold holder. Pour the compound back and forth between mold holder and container several times to fill all crevices. When the liquid hardens, it becomes the mold.

Figure A: Cardboard tube extensions, inserted in holes left in the plaster by the clay horns, allow more mold-holder compound to be poured in, increasing pressure to force compound around model.

12: After the plaster mold holder is removed, the flexible mold is sliced open to release the model. Cuts are made in center of mold's thickened perimeter.

13: After the flexible mold is sliced apart, it is carefully pulled away from the sculpted model to avoid damaging it. The model is then removed.

14: Each half of the flexible mold is replaced in its matching plaster mold holder. Inspect the inside of the mold; remove any bits of clay that have stuck.

cures. When it has set, it will be dry but flexible, even rubbery. Open the mold holder again, cutting off the compound that penetrated the drilled air vents, to facilitate removal. Just leave the compound in the holes.

The most delicate operation of the project comes next: cutting the flexible mold apart to remove the model, as in photographs 12 and 13. With a very sharp tool—I used a surgeon's scalpel, but a modeler's replaceable-blade knife will do—slice into the center of the thickened ridge. Work all the way around the ridge, and include the horns made by the pouring tubes. Cut carefully in a series of small slices, gradually increasing depth of slice. But be careful not to cut into the clay model inside. As you get nearly through the flexible mold, pull the rubber to stretch it away from the model as you slice. Once you have cut through in one place, it is easier to work

427

15: Mold holder, with flexible mold inside, is clamped and ready to receive the casting plaster. Here, U-shape metal bars clamp the mold holder together, but C-clamps or clothesline would also work.

16: Fresh casting plaster is mixed for pouring into the mold. It is sifted into the water as described on page 424, then mixed to a creamlike consistency. Mold is turned bottom up for the pour.

17: Brace the mold holder with wood blocks, bricks or sandbags while plaster is poured in. Mix enough plaster to fill the mold. Start pouring immediately after mixing, before plaster can harden.

18: Pour the plaster back and forth between mold and container several times. This helps fill all the crevices inside the mold and eliminate air pockets. Each time the mold is filled, shake it gently.

19: Remove the plaster casting when it has hardened. Unclamp the mold holder, and pull away the mold. Its flexibility will bend around undercut areas, which might lock with a more rigid mold.

your way around, stretching and cutting as you go. Make sure you have cut the rubber all the way around the perimeter of the mold, so that the two halves come apart like halves of a grapefruit. These halves form the actual mold. Remove the model and its plaster base. They are no longer needed for this project. Inspect the inside surface of the flexible mold carefully. Remove any particles of clay that may have come from the model. Be careful not to mar or tear any of the delicate ridges or crevices in the mold. These preserve the precise details of the original model.

Making the Final Casting
Place each flexible-mold half back in its plaster mold holder, as in photograph 14, page 427. Be sure each is seated perfectly. Then fit the halves of the plaster mold holder together, and clamp them, as in photograph 15. Use the U-clamps or C-clamps as you did before, but this time you will not have to seal the side cracks with clay. The plaster will not work out through the tightly clamped seams of the flexible mold.

Turn the mold over, open end up, and brace it securely on the work surface. Now you are ready to make your first plaster casting. Follow the plaster-mixing procedure described on page 424, and mix 5 pounds of plaster to fill the mold cavity (photograph 16). It should be mixed to a consistency slightly thicker than heavy cream. Pour the plaster into the mold and then back and forth between the mixing bowl and the mold several times. You should also swirl it around in the mold, to make sure it gets into all the intricate nooks and crannies of the mold. Finally, fill the mold to the top (figure B). Brace the mold carefully so it will remain level and secure while the plaster hardens. Then leave the mold overnight or, better, a full day to allow the plaster to thoroughly cure and harden.

To extract the cast from the mold, remove the clamps, and pry open the mold holder as for the previous openings. Then remove the cast from the mold. It is not likely that there will be any mold marks; but if there are, scrape them away with a spatula or a fingernail. Inspect the cast carefully, and fill any air bubbles you find with wet plaster. Let the cast air-dry for a day or so while the surface hardens. If the cast feels even slightly damp or cool against your face, it is not dry.

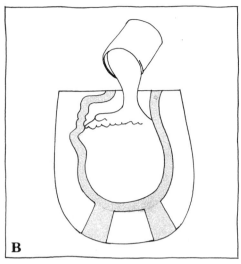

Figure B: With mold turned upside down and well braced, plaster is poured into bottom opening, then poured back and forth several times between mold and container to make sure it gets into all the crannies of the mold.

20: The plaster cast is finished by shellacking, rubbing with shoe polish to bring out relief, adding bronze powder for highlights, coating with paste wax and buffing lightly.

Finishing the Cast

The final step, when the cast is completely dry, is to finish it. Here, you can pretty much let your imagination be your guide. The cast can be simply sealed with shellac if you wish. Or it can be spray painted with automotive spray finish, antiqued, waxed, or even stained. My choice was to seal the plaster with shellac and then apply rubbed-on brown shoe polish, thinned with a little benzene, as in photograph 20. The finish was then rubbed gently to bring out the relief; too much rubbing dulls the edges of the cast. Bronze powder was then dusted on and gently rubbed to produce attractive highlights. Finally, a coat of paste wax, warmed in a double boiler to make it thinner, was applied and buffed slightly with a soft cloth. The final effect achieved is that of a warm, glowing, metallic patina.

Mounting the Cast

Although the bust in this project did not necessarily call for mounting on a base, that can easily be done. Leave the mounting surface free of finish, and apply two-part epoxy glue. Then glue it to a wood or marble base, cut to a size appropriate for your sculpture. The base should not be so large or bulky that it dominates the sculpture, which is, after all, what you want people to notice first. You probably can cut and finish a wood base yourself. If you want marble, a local supplier of headstones can cut one for you.

Carving and Molding
Casting a belt buckle $$ ⌧ 🚶 ⚗

A metal belt buckle cast by the lost-wax process can be as simple or as elaborate as you wish. To make it, you will need about 5 pounds of casting plaster, half of a 1½-by-9½-by-11¾-inch block of sculptor's or modeling wax (paraffin will not do), and 5 pounds of tin (look under Tin or Scrap Metals in the yellow pages of your telephone directory). Tin can be melted on a kitchen stove, retains details crisply, and, when used for a belt buckle, looks much like silver.

Sketch the outlines of the belt buckle and your design to fit within those outlines. Figure C shows my version. Then cut off a piece of sculptor's wax, and warm it between your hands. Pat the warmed wax into a slab ⅛ to ⅜ inch thick and large enough for you to cut the length and width of the buckle from it. With a sharp knife, cut the outlines of the buckle from the slab. Then, with the knife or a sharp pencil, incise in the front of the wax buckle any background designs you wish to add. If you would like to imprint background textures on any areas of the design (using a wire screen, for example), this is the time to do it. Bend the slab so its outside is slightly convex, to fit the curvature of the waistline.

Add the relief components of the design to the front of the buckle by sticking small bits of wax on the buckle slab. In the case of the flower design shown, the center and each petal were separate pieces of wax, pressed into place and shaped. Even though some of these protrude and are curved, they will be reproduced faithfully in the metal. For the belt loop, roll a small piece of wax into a cylinder about ⅛ to ¼ inch in diameter. This can be attached to one end of the buckle, as shown below, or fixed at right angles to the back of the buckle. In the latter case, the tail end of the belt will come through the loop again and end on the outside. In the former case, the tail end will be under the belt and fastened with a pin fitting through a hole in the belt.

If you place the belt loop on the end of the buckle as I did, the necessary small pin in the end opposite the loop, on the back, cannot be molded as part of the buckle, because plain tin is not strong enough. Make the buckle slab slightly thicker where the pin will mount (see figure D) to provide reinforcing

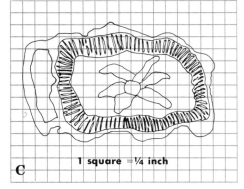

Figure C: Pattern for the belt buckle shown in the color photograph.

1 square = ¼ inch

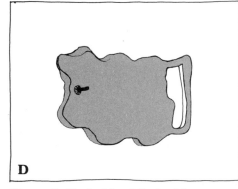

Figure D: Back side of the buckle, showing the location of the pin that fastens into a hole in the belt.

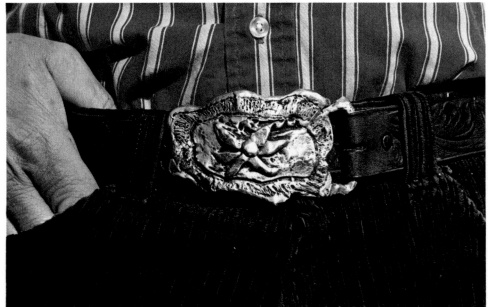

This belt buckle was originally created in sculptor's wax and then cast in solid tin by the lost-wax method. The work was done in an ordinary kitchen.

for mounting a steel pin in the buckle (one of the last steps). You thicken the area where the pin will mount by pressing a piece of wax, half the size of a pea, onto the back of the buckle slab. Smooth its edges into the wax of the buckle body, but don't press it too flat.

When the buckle modeled in wax is completed, it is necessary to build with wax the passageways that will let the molten metal reach the buckle and also let trapped air escape. The larger passageways are called runners, and the smaller ones are called air vents. At the top of the main vertical runner, a waxed paper cup is attached to create an enlarged pouring hole, called a sprue. The runners, air vents, and sprue are assembled into the treelike structure shown in figure E. Remember that everything you make of wax will be a cavity in the final mold. The purpose is to permit the molten metal to flow easily into all parts of the mold and to let the air and gases escape so they won't make voids or bubbles in the casting.

The runners and air vents can be formed out of warm wax, or buy wax rods and sticks from a craft-supply outlet and cut them to appropriate lengths. Make the main runner and the two short ones from a wax stick ½ to ¾ inch in diameter. The short runners will support the wax buckle. Attach the two side runners at right angles to the main runner, as in figure E.

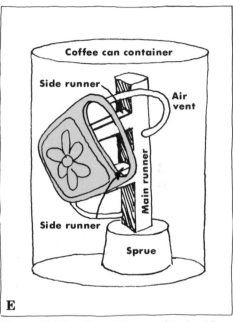

E

21: Make the body of the wax buckle by softening wax in palms, shaping into a slab, and cutting out. Then incise background designs on buckle surface.

22: Add flower design by making the center and each petal separately, then pressing in place while soft. Then form belt loop, and attach it to one end.

Figure E: Wax "tree" fastened to buckle model. This is how the wax buckle and its supports are placed in a container before the plaster that forms the mold is cast.

23: Container placed around the wax structure will hold the casting plaster that forms the mold. Both container ends are open. The container's bottom is sealed to a board with modeling clay so the plaster you pour will not work its way out.

24: Mix casting plaster to a creamy consistency, and pour into the container around the wax model and over it, making sure to fill every nook and cranny. Fill the container to the top. Let mold dry out several days before proceeding.

25: Place the dry plaster mold in a 170F oven for several hours to melt out the wax model inside it. Use a drip pan below it to catch melting wax. Empty the pan at frequent intervals.

26: Tin can be melted in a cast-iron pot on top of the stove. Stir and melt in 3 feet of 12-gauge copper wire to give the tin added strength. The process of melting the tin takes about half an hour.

The wax model of the buckle and its wax supports are perfectly reproduced in hard metal. This is a simple design, but quite intricate castings can be made by the lost-wax method.

The technique of attaching or welding wax pieces to each other is applying a hot knife to joining areas, then pressing them together. Weld the inside of the buckle slab to the ends of the short runners, as shown in figure E, page 431. Now roll out two ⅛-inch-diameter wax rods. Attach one to a top corner of the buckle and the other to a bottom corner of the buckle, and bend them so they can be attached to the main runner (see figure E). These are the passageways that help prevent air and molten wax from being trapped inside the buckle mold.

For the pouring hole or sprue, place a small waxed paper cup, upside down, on a wax-coated card or piece of metal. Seal the bottom of the wax stick that is the main runner to the bottom of the cup, as in figure E.

The treelike wax structure must now be encased in plaster to make the mold. You will need to place a container around the wax structure to hold the plaster you will pour. Use a two-pound coffee can with both ends removed for a container. Put the wax structure on a piece of wood, and place the container over it. Seal the base of the container to the wood with modeling clay.

Now mix 5 pounds of casting plaster according to the instructions on page 424. Pour it around the wax structure, using a brisk and continuous motion so every crevice and corner of the wax model will be filled. Let the plaster air-dry for at least three or four days. When dry, it will not feel cold or damp against your skin.

To melt the wax out of the plaster mold, place the mold, opening down, in a

27: Pour the molten metal into the mold, which was already preheated to melt out wax. Use a steady pouring motion. Place the mold on scrap plywood to minimize any damage if the metal spatters.

28: After pouring the molten metal, let it cool for an hour. Then place the mold in a bucket of cold water. Water softens the plaster, which you then chip away from the casting with hammer and chisel.

shallow container, and place both in the kitchen oven. Heat oven to about 170F, but no higher. Check frequently, and as melted wax accumulates in the pan, empty it. At this temperature, there is little danger, but there could be unpleasant odors if wax accumulated. When no more wax comes out, turn the mold on its side, and let it heat another hour. Then turn it upside down again, and heat for another hour, to remove trapped pockets of wax. Turn it on the other side, and heat again for an hour. When no more wax can be coaxed out, turn the mold upside down again, and turn the oven up to 400F, to burn out residual wax that has soaked into the plaster. Heat for about an hour.

As the mold heating is going on, prepare for the metal pouring. Place chunks of tin in a cast-iron pot, and place pot on a stove burner at high heat. It will take about half an hour to bring the metal to melting point.

In handling molten tin or lead, wear asbestos fireplace gloves or use enough potholders to insulate against the heat for at least two minutes. Some metal might splatter in pouring, so it is wise to wear protective safety glasses, high-top leather shoes, and long pants tied around the ankles.

When the metal is molten, remove the plaster mold from the oven, and place it on a 2-foot-square piece of plywood, on the floor. Seat the mold securely

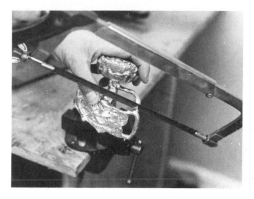

29: With a hacksaw, cut off the excess metal left by the vents and pouring gates. Hold work securely in a vise, and cut as close as possible to the buckle. Save the excess metal for future castings.

30: File away remaining excess metal from the buckle back. Finish the cuts with fine aluminum-oxide abrasive paper. To make hooking pin, drill a pilot hole for a small screw; insert it, and cut off head.

31: Finish the metal casting of the buckle by rubbing with fine steel wool, then rubbing with an emery cloth. To bring out the relief of the design, rub black shoe polish into the crevices, and wipe away the excess.

with the cup opening (sprue) facing up. Poise the melting pot's pouring spout or lip over the opening, and pour in one continuous motion until the mold is full to the top of the cup hole with molten metal.

Let the mold stand for an hour before trying to remove the casting. The metal will solidify in minutes, but will remain dangerously hot much longer. After an hour, pick up the mold with potholders, and place it in a bucket of cold water. This will both cool the metal and soften the plaster mold. Remove the coffee-can container, and with hammer and chisel, carefully chip away the plaster. Work from the sprue downward and take care not to damage the metal parts. Use an ice pick to remove any plaster in crevices.

Next, install the retaining pin in the buckle, (figure D). Drill a ⅛-inch hole about halfway through the buckle, from the inside. The pin is a No. 6 by 1-inch steel screw. Cut off the threaded point so the length of the remaining threads equals the depth of the hole. With a screwdriver, turn the screw into the hole. It will cut its own threads in the soft metal. Use a hacksaw to cut off screw's shank ⅜ inch from the buckle. File cut end round and smooth.

Polish the buckle with fine-grade steel wool. Then rub black shoe polish into the background details to bring out the design. Wipe off excess, and polish again. Spray with water-clear lacquer to preserve the luster.

For related projects and crafts, see the entries "Acrylics," "Belts and Buckles," "Buttons," "Jewelry," and "Sand-Casting."

Unglazed tile at left was imprinted with a leaf before drying and firing. Rolling rope over a flat tile created diagonal pattern on tile in background. On the two tiles with white backgrounds, colored glaze patterns were applied over dried white glazes. Tiles shown on the cover of this volume were made using the basic techniques given on the following pages.

CERAMICS

Commencing with Clay

Working with clay is one of man's oldest crafts. Even before recorded history, man had discovered how easy it is to shape useful and beautiful objects from this material that is plastic when it is moist. When it has dried, it becomes hard enough to hold its shape indefinitely. Firing it in a kiln gives it a stonelike durability that can last for centuries, as the many tile and pottery pieces left by ancient civilizations attest.

The resistance of fired clay (ceramics) to water, salt, acids, heat, and cold also makes it an ideal material for containing food and drink. But it is the ease with which clay can be formed into varied shapes—and decorated with myriad colors of glazes—that attracts the craftsman. Even beginners can enjoy making the colorful tiles, bowls, and openwork coat hooks shown on the opposite and following pages.

While the primitive potter had to make do with the clay he found along the river bed, today's home ceramist has a variety of premixed clays available. These divide into three basic types. The first clays are the coarser-textured ones used to make earthenware; they can be fired at 1800 to 2100F to help bond them, but they will still remain porous. The second clays are those used to make stoneware; these can be fired at a higher temperature (2100 to 2300F), so that they vitrify and lose porosity. The third clays are used to make porcelain; these can be fired at 2250 to 2500F to produce the translucency typical of fine china.

The porcelain clays are less pliable and harder to work with, and they are more liable to crack or explode when fired. Both the earthenware and stoneware clays are easy to work. Of the two, the stoneware clays are less porous and more durable. So, for the projects that follow, I recommend the use of stoneware clays.

You can make all the projects in this entry from one 25-pound block of clay, which is approximately a foot square and costs only a few dollars. Ceramic-supply stores and studios, and some hobby shops and department stores, stock this size. Make sure the block you buy has been kept sealed and moist in an airtight plastic wrap. If the store doesn't know whether it is a stoneware clay, check the label; if this indicates a firing range between "cone 06 and 6" (see page 438), the clay is for stoneware.

Clay also comes in many colors, an important factor if you plan to leave a piece uncolored by glaze. Ask at the store to see sample chips showing the various colors of clay before and after firing.

Martha Longenecker is a noted artist-craftsperson in ceramics and a professor of art at California State University, San Diego. A graduate of UCLA and recipient of a Master of Fine Arts degree from California's Claremont Graduate School and University Center, Professor Longenecker has traveled twice around the world, studying and collecting pottery and related folk art.

Ceramics
Making clay tiles

The tiles shown in the color photograph opposite were cut from rolled-out slabs of clay. To cut out 15 tiles similar to those shown, you need, in addition to the clay, two 22-inch lengths of 1-by-½-inch wood strips to form the edges of the clay slab from which the tiles are cut. You also need a 16-inch length of 1-inch dowel, which is used to roll out the slab; a 24-inch ruler; a plastic triangle; and a dull kitchen paring knife.

The first step in making the tiles is preparing the clay. You should add a ground-up fired clay, called grog, to the fresh clay. The grog makes the clay more porous, helping any air bubbles in the clay escape. In rolling out slabs, inexperienced ceramists frequently leave small air bubbles in the clay. These bubbles may later explode during firing, ruining the project. You can purchase clay with grog already mixed into it, or mix your own. Grog

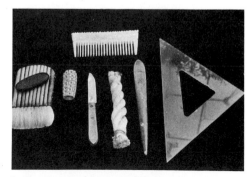

1: Some suggested equipment to use in beginning to explore ceramics includes wide, soft brush, smooth stone (resting on brush), ceramic bead with raised pattern for imprinting, dull paring knife, comb, segment of rope, pointed clay-modeling tool, and plastic triangle. Ceramic-supply outlets carry modeling tools and ceramic beads or other objects to be used for imprinting. (Other equipment will be noted as it is needed for particular projects.)

is available from the same ceramic-supply outlets that stock clay, and one measuring cup of grog is ample for kneading into 25 pounds of clay. But take the time to make sure the grog and fresh clay are well blended.

The clay mixture for the tiles should not be so stiff that it cracks when you bend a piece of it. It should not have any lumps or hard pieces. It should not be sticky, but just soft enough so you can mold and form it with your fingers. Working on oilcloth that has the face side down, knead the clay until it is the right consistency. If it is too hard and dry, add water, and work it into the mix.

When the mix is the right consistency, you are ready to make the slab for the tiles. Position the two 1-by-½ inch wood strips parallel to each other and 12 inches apart, with the ½-inch dimensions facing. If you have laid your oilcloth on a good table, put a piece of scrap wood under the cloth to protect the table surface. Next, pinch off a handful of the clay mix, as in photograph 2, and push it down against the oilcloth between the two wood strips. Press the clay down hard with the heel of your hand, as in photograph 3, to eliminate any trapped air. Continue adding handfuls of clay, pressing them down and smoothing them until you have filled the space between the wood strips and have formed a rough clay slab. The slab should be about 21 or 22 inches long and ¾ inch high, extending slightly above the wood strips.

Now place the length of dowel across the two wood strips, and begin rolling it back and forth over the clay to even the surface, as in photograph 4. Rolling will be somewhat difficult at first, but it becomes easier as the clay levels out. If the clay begins to accumulate on the dowel, scrape it off before doing any more rolling.

When your slab has been rolled to a uniform thickness and its surface is smooth, run the paring knife along the edges, between the clay and the wood

2: When the clay mixture is the right consistency (see text), pinch off a handful, and press it down on a work surface covered with face-down oilcloth.

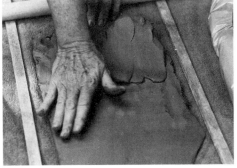

3: Press clay down between two side strips, using heel of hand to force out trapped air. Continue adding clay until area between the wood strips is filled.

4: Press firmly as you roll dowel back and forth until the slab has a uniform thickness and smooth surface. Scrape clay pieces off dowel if they accumulate.

5: After squaring off end of slab, using a plastic triangle and ruler or wood side strip, cut through clay with a paring knife, as shown. Use side strip as guide.

6: Remove side strips, and with triangle and ruler, divide slab into 15 4-inch squares. Cut out tile squares, using the triangle or ruler for a cutting guide.

7: Gather clay scraps left from trimming slab; press into a ball; put in a plastic bag, and seal the bag. If clay has dried, moisten it before sealing the bag.

Ceramic tiles do not have to have flat surfaces. They can be textured in a variety of interesting ways, as these tiles suggest.

strips, to free the strips from the clay. Next, square off one end of the slab. Use the plastic triangle and the ruler or one of the side strips to make sure the line you mark is at right angles to the sides of the slab. Working close to the end of the slab, mark the end line lightly with the tip of the paring-knife blade. Then, using the ruler or wood strip as a firmly held guide, cut through the clay with the knife as in photograph 5. Next, measure and mark 20 inches from the end of the slab you have just cut. Use the knife point to lightly incise a line that runs through this mark at right angles to the sides of the slab. This line marks the other end of the slab. Cut it as you did the first end.

With the sides and ends of the 12-by-20-inch slab established, divide the slab into 4-inch squares. Use the ruler and triangle, as you did for the slab ends, to make sure horizontal and vertical lines are at right angles to each other. Next, using the ruler or triangle as a guide, cut through the clay along these lines with the paring knife, as in photograph 6.

Before decorating the tiles, gather the scraps of clay left from cutting out the tiles (photograph 7); slap them together to keep air from being trapped within, and press them into a ball. Place the ball in a sealed plastic bag for later use. If the clay has become too hard to work easily, poke holes in it, and knead in some water before sealing the clay in the bag.

As an alternative to the flat slab and the flat tiles it produces, you might try a variation like that shown in photograph 8. Or try rolling a short section of stout rope over a flat tile (see color photograph, page 434). Other texture variations are shown in the color photograph above. You can also trace and cut different shapes of tiles (see the cover of this volume).

8: Instead of using a smooth surface, roll out the clay slab on a woven mat to achieve interesting texture on the front or back. You can roll out clay on any woven fabric, macrame, or nonstick material that has an unusual texture.

9: To decorate tile before firing, brush slip, made by thinning a contrastingly colored clay with water, over wet tile. Cut through slip to make what is termed a sgraffito design (photograph 10).

10: Use an orange stick to make lines; cut through the light-colored slip so dark clay shows through and forms an interesting geometric pattern that can be repeated on other tiles (photograph 11).

11: Scratch identical designs on four tiles. Place together, sides touching. Use stick to redefine the lines; then roll the surfaces with a piece of doweling to soften the pattern. Next, the tiles are air-dried, then bisque fired.

After you have formed the tiles, they must be air-dried before being fired. This is true of all clay projects, however they are made. Flat pieces such as tiles should be placed on newspaper or some other porous material to dry, and turned occasionally to prevent warpage. As the moisture evaporates from the clay, the tiles shrink, usually between 10 and 15 percent. Keep this in mind if relatively accurate dimensions are needed for the finished product. (For example, to make sure your 15 tiles would be quite close to 4 inches square after they had dried, you would have had to use a 13½-by-22½-inch slab of clay and divided it equally into 15 squares. But such precision is not usually required.) Once the tiles are totally dry, to a leather-hard consistency, they are ready to be fired.

There are some methods of decorating tiles that you can use before firing, indeed even before the tiles are dry. One is to brush a thin coat of a contrasting color of liquid clay, called slip, over the still-wet tiles, as in photograph 9. Then use an orange stick from a manicure set to cut a design through the slip, so the contrasting color of the original tile shows through, as in photographs 10 and 11. You can mix your own slip by simply thinning clay with water until it has a creamy consistency. (In contrast, the slip used for joining the clay pieces on pages 441 through 445 is thick and pastelike.)

Firing the Clay

Firing ceramics serves two purposes: It permanently bonds the clay, and it melts and fuses glazes onto clay surfaces. But the two processes are usually achieved in separate steps involving two firings. The first firing, which takes about eight to ten hours, is called the bisque or biscuit firing; the second, which takes six to ten hours, is called the gloss or glaze firing. If glaze will not be used, the clay can be decorated with slip when wet, then air-dried and fired only once (bisque fired). It is also possible to glaze a clay piece before it is bisque fired; but the two-step firing is more generally used when glazes are involved, because it allows better control of the clay and the glaze colors.

Firing is done in a kiln (pronounced kill), which is an oven furnace used for ceramic work of all types. While home kilns may be purchased from ceramic-supply outlets, they are expensive ($125 and up), and the techniques of firing are complex. Kilns must be loaded in a special way, and the firing times and temperatures vary with the type of ware and the kind of firing, either bisque or glaze. For these reasons, the beginning ceramist is better off using the firing services provided by commercial studios and ceramics-supply outlets. These places charge a modest fee based on the size and number of pieces and the temperature at which they are to be fired. You can keep the cost down by having stoneware pieces fired at lower earthenware temperatures; but the fired pieces will then be more porous than if they had been fired at the higher stoneware temperatures.

Ceramic pieces should never be fired at a higher temperature than the upper limit specified for the type of clay used. For earthenware, this would be 2100F; for stoneware, 2300F. If fired above these temperature limits, the clay piece will melt and deform.

To monitor temperatures achieved in firing, pyrometric cones are placed in the kiln. These are so made that they melt at specific temperatures, signaling that the temperature inside the kiln has reached that temperature.

The cone designations on the labels of many prepackaged clays indicate their firing ranges. Thus, cones 022 through 01 indicate low-fire earthenware; cones 1 through 5 indicate earthenware and stoneware; cone 6, stoneware to be fired at 2232F; and cones 7 through 12, stoneware and porcelain.

Glazing

After pieces have been bisque fired, they are ready for glazing. Glaze is a glasslike coating that is melted and fused to the surface of clay. Glazes are made from inorganic substances like lead, soda, borax, and feldspar, mixed

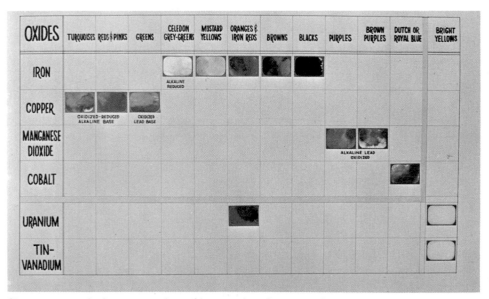

OXIDES	TURQUOISES	REDS & PINKS	GREENS	CELEDON GREY-GREENS	MUSTARD YELLOWS	ORANGES & IRON REDS	BROWNS	BLACKS	PURPLES	BROWN PURPLES	DUTCH OR ROYAL BLUE	BRIGHT YELLOWS
IRON				▢ ALKALINE REDUCED	▢	▢	▢	▢				
COPPER	▢	▢ OXIDIZED-REDUCED ALKALINE BASE	▢ OXIDIZED LEAD BASE									
MANGANESE DIOXIDE									▢	▢ ALKALINE LEAD OXIDIZED		
COBALT											▢	
URANIUM						▢						▢
TIN-VANADIUM												▢

Glazes are made from a number of inorganic substances that are mixed with various metallic oxides to produce different colors. This chart illustrates the range of glaze colors it is possible to achieve by varying the metallic oxides that are used.

with metallic oxides for color. An almost infinite variety of colors and textural effects can be achieved. The chart above, furnished by San Diego State University in California, shows a variety of colors made possible by combinations of metallic oxides used in glaze preparation. In addition to the different oxides used, glaze is affected by many other variables, including the type of clay being glazed and the kiln temperature.

Glaze can be mixed to a creamy consistency for brushing over clay, or thinned with water for dipping, spraying, or pouring over clay surfaces. As a general guideline, for tile decoration the glaze should be brushed on until it is the thickness of a dime.

The white-and-blue tiles pictured on page 434 illustrate one popular method of applying glaze to achieve a special effect. A coat of white glaze is first brushed over the bisque-fired tiles. When the glaze has dried enough to lose its sheen, the additional colors (in this case, blue and yellow) are brushed on in the design desired. The tiles are then glaze fired.

Another popular technique for glazing bisque-fired tiles is called the wax-resist method. First, a design is painted on the tile, as in photograph 12, with a liquid wax you can obtain from a ceramic-supply outlet. The waxed areas will not absorb glaze applied over them, hence the name wax-resist. Next, a thin layer of prepared cobalt-and-iron glaze is brushed over the whole tile, as in photograph 13. The glaze is allowed to dry and then is fired. The waxed pattern will show through quite clearly in the finished piece after firing.

In applying glaze, make sure none of it gets on the back of the tiles. This would make them stick to the kiln shelves during firing.

Sources for Glaze

The beginning ceramist would do well to consult with a ceramic studio or a ceramic-supply outlet on the types of glaze needed to achieve certain effects and how the glazes should be applied. These sources can also supply the glazes, which usually come in powdered form. They can be mixed with water and applied at home. Once you have applied a glaze, the sources may be able to do the glaze firing for you for a fee. Do *not* use homemade glazes for food and drink containers; make sure the glaze is one that has been tested and approved as safe for these articles.

12: To decorate tiles with the wax-resist method, with a soft brush paint a design in liquid wax (from ceramic-supply store) on a bisque-fired tile. Waxed areas will not absorb glaze applied over them. Let wax dry a few minutes before glazing.

13: After painting design on tile with liquid wax, brush a thin layer of prepared cobalt-and-iron glaze over the entire tile. Notice how flower design shows through the glaze. Let glaze dry a few minutes. Then have glazed tile fired.

Ceramics
Making a clay bowl

A shallow clay bowl can be made by adding another technique to those already learned in making simple tiles. After you have rolled out an even clay slab, using the strip-and-dowel method (photographs 2 through 4, page 436) cut out an 8-by-12-inch oval freehand. Imprint a design on it; then place it on a plastic-covered pillow, and adjust it to the desired curvature. You can also use a sling, basket, or sand to support the clay. Do not remove the bowl until the clay holds its shape (becomes leather-hard). This usually takes several days, longer if the weather is damp or cool.

Use a dull table knife to trim or scrape the edges and remove any rough spots. Burnish (shine) the surface with a smooth stone. Cut a handle as in figure A. Let dry thoroughly, then bisque fire at a stoneware temperature. Brush glaze over the inside; then remove excess with paper toweling, leaving glaze only in the grooves if you have chosen to add them. Perform glaze firing. Depending on the type of glaze applied, the bowl can be used as a serving dish or as a wall decoration.

14: Draw freehand and cut an oval, about 8 by 12 inches, from a ½-inch-thick clay slab. With a wide hair comb, swirl texture through the center of the form. The bowl can be made any size you wish.

15: Place the imprinted clay oval in a depression in a plastic-covered pillow. Arrange pillow until the curvature of the bowl pleases you. Don't remove the bowl until clay reaches a leather-hard stage.

16: To polish or burnish the bowl, first dampen the surface. Then rub with a smooth stone to push all small particles below the surface, leaving a satiny finish. Bowl can now be bisque fired.

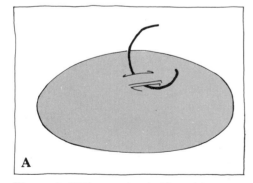

A

Figure A: With a paring knife, cut two shallow half-circle indentations in back of bowl. Use wire to remove clay between lower portions of half circles, leaving a bridge that forms a handle, as shown.

It is only one more step from making a tile to making a decorative, useful bowl.

Ceramics
Making a coiled bowl

$ 🕐 🚶 🔥

Making containers with coils of clay is an ancient method utilized by artisans long before the invention of the potter's wheel. Ceramic pieces that leave many spaces, like the bowl made with coils, are called openwork. I enjoy this type of work because the product is lighter and more delicate than solid-clay work. Everything except the firing can be done in your kitchen, garage, or back yard.

Stoneware clay is recommended for both coil projects—the bowl and the

This ceramic bowl is made of interlocking repetitions of a simple flower shape. Elements are cemented together with a thin mixture of clay and water, called slip.

Paula Johansson was born in Finland and raised in Sweden, where she trained for a career in commercial art and design. Later, while she was studying at the Laguna Beach School of Art, her interests turned to ceramics. Currently she creates ceramic pieces for sale at the Sawdust Festival and Winter Art Festival, both held at Laguna Beach.

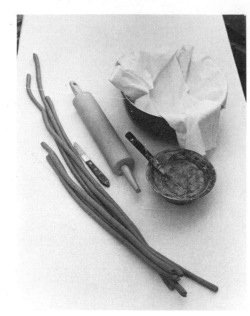

17: Materials used in openwork projects: rolled clay strips; knife for cutting; rolling pin; kitchen fork for scoring pieces to be slipped together, shown here in a bowl of slip; and large bowl and fabric, within which clay bowl is formed. You will also need a container for mixing glazes.

coat hooks on pages 444 and 445. Work with clay hard enough to keep its shape but soft enough to be rolled easily into rounded strips. Roll several 2-foot-long strips by hand. Coil them to form five-petaled flowers, each 5 inches in diameter. As you form a flower (photograph 19), press center lightly with a rolling pin. This pushes center firmly together and flattens it slightly, making flower uniform in depth. In a kitchen bowl about 12 inches in diameter and 6 to 8 inches deep, put a piece of fabric. Place one flower shape in the bottom of the bowl; add the others one at a time. Joining pieces before they are fired requires thick slip, clay mixed with water to a pastelike consistency. Although there are tools designed for slipping (joining), I prefer an old table fork. Use the tines to scratch or roughen surfaces that will touch. Dab slip on these areas, and push the pieces firmly together. Remove excess slip with your finger or the fork. Parts of any assembled clay project must always be well slipped together to keep them from separating during firing. Continue slipping flower shapes together in the bowl until the inside is covered. Let dry until the clay is leather-hard. With the fabric, lift clay bowl out of the kitchen bowl. Make a base by coiling a strip to make a double circle 5 inches in diameter. Roll several clay balls, and flatten them on outside of coils for decoration. Slip the bowl onto the base. Let dry several days. Have the bowl bisque fired at a stoneware temperature.

In separate containers, mix prepared powdered glazes with water to a creamy consistency. Dip the bowl into matte-white glaze, keeping the bottom free of glaze. Pieces stick if any glaze comes in contact with the kiln shelf during firing. Let glaze dry until it loses its sheen; then dip bowl into cobalt-blue glaze before glaze firing. This was done with the blue bowl shown opposite.

18: Form a ½-inch-thick strip by rolling out clay on the working surface. Use the palms of your hands to do the rolling.

19: Loop a clay strip around to form a five-petaled flower. Press down where clay overlaps at the flower's center.

20: Join flower shapes in bowl with slip. Each flower should touch others on at least three surfaces for strength.

21: Hold the bowl carefully as you lower it onto the prepared double-coil clay base. Bowl and base are joined with slip.

▶ Openwork ceramic bowls are colored with white and blue glazes. Repeated dipping in glazes intensifies the color.

▲ You can arrange the basic coiled-clay element to create many designs for sturdy coat hooks. Nail for hanging goes through open loop opposite the hook.

22: Form curl shapes by rolling a strip toward the center from both ends. As you finish each curled piece, place it in position with the others to make certain that all are similar in size.

Ceramics
Coat hooks

Familiarity with coil work will enable you to use the technique for other simple projects like these ceramic coat hooks. Work with clay soft enough to be easily rolled and coiled. To make a four-sided hook, start with four 1-foot-long strips of clay rolled out to ½ inch in diameter. Mark the center of each. Starting at one end of a strip, roll it to the center to form a curl. Then roll from the other end until the curls touch. Make four curled segments, and place in position, as in photograph 22. Join the pieces with slip. Roll several small clay balls about ½ inch in diameter, and slip these on all touching joints, pressing each firmly into position as in photograph 23. Coils tend to unwind as they air-dry. The small spheres prevent unwinding and also give necessary strength at joints. Form the hook (photograph 24); place one end behind a curl, and slip the pieces together. Add a loop opposite the hook. Let dry; then bisque fire.

Ceramic hooks may be glazed in the same manner as the coiled bowl (see pages 442 and 443). First, dip in matte-white glaze. Let dry about 5 minutes; then dip in cobalt-blue glaze. Be sure to dip only the front two-thirds of the hook in glaze, so the back (which will rest on the kiln shelf) is glaze-free. Then glaze fire. All hooks pictured above were dipped into white or cobalt-blue glaze. Color variations were achieved by redipping several times in one or both colors or by dipping first in blue, then in white. For small amounts of surface color, dip in one color; paint on second sparingly.

23: Place slip between all touching edges and under each small clay sphere. Press the spheres firmly into position.

24: Cut a 4-inch-long rolled strip; double it; place in position for hook. Bend one end up into desired position.

25: Dip front of the coiled coat hook in matte-white glaze. Quantity of glaze is for dipping hooks and bowls on page 443.

These coil projects will give you a feeling for working with clay in this manner. They are by no means all you can do with clay coils. Experiment with thicker and thinner coils and different glaze colors. You can shape coils into cylinders, built around an oatmeal box; squares, built around a cardboard box; or curved forms, built over a bowl. Other projects might include sconces, trivets, and decorative picture frames.

For related projects, see the entries "Buttons," "Enameling," "Kilns," "Mosaics," "Pottery," and "Tiles."

CHEESES AND CHURNING
Natural Dairy Products

Freda Baron Friedman is the editor of the Journal of Practical Nursing and has written and edited many articles about nutrition. An inveterate cheese eater, she takes special pleasure in making her own.

For thousands of years, people the world over have been making milk products that bear little or no resemblance to milk. Many of these are the result of fermentation. Others, such as butter and mayonnaise, depend on churning or beating to convert them from cream (as in butter) and egg yolks (as in mayonnaise) to their final state.

Making these foods at home, in much the way our ancestors did, is in itself interesting, and they are nutritionally valuable additions to the diet, as they are rich in vitamins and minerals. Since these homemade products do not contain any preservatives, natural-food purists consider them especially healthful. In any case, the flavors are fresh and excellent.

Basic equipment you will need to make cheeses and dairy products is found in most kitchens. You will need a cooking thermometer with calibrations from 90 to 120F and a few yards of cheesecloth which is sold in packages by supermarkets and hardware stores. If you go in for the making of hard cheese then you will have to improvise, or make a cheese press. A double-boiler, and wooden spoons, are also useful, but you can also use metal spoons and place a small pot set in a larger one to simulate a double boiler. Recipes begin below.

Kitchen Favorites and Celebrations
Yogurts and sour cream

Making yogurt is a good way to start to learn cheesemaking. Though yogurt is not a cheese, the fermentation process responsible for yogurt is similar to the first step in making many soft cheeses. With the fermentation process, you can make all sorts of dairy products, from cottage cheese to sour cream. The recipe for Basic Yogurt is given on page 448.

Yogurt depends on the growth of bacteria to form lactic acid. When milk is inoculated with one or more types of the yogurt bacteria, they begin to grow, forming lactic acid and killing any harmful bacteria that may have infected the milk. The milk used differs from area to area, as do the bacteria. In the United States, cow's milk is used; in Armenia, buffalo's or goat's milk; in Lapland, reindeer's or mare's milk. Flavor and consistency vary with the type of milk and the bacteria.

A Historic Food
Yogurt has been the diet of peasants and the delicacy of kings for more than four thousand years. Throughout history there have been rituals and rules about yogurt. In some countries, cultures of bacteria were passed down from generation to generation, as part of a girl's dowry. Legend tells that Genghis Khan fed his vast army on yogurt to give the men strength during their long marches through the Orient and Persia. Other legends have linked yogurt consumption with long life, virility, the restoration of thinning hair, and the treatment of ulcers and other stomach ailments. Persian women were reported to preserve the freshness of their skin by eating yogurt and using it as a facial cream. Even today, some people believe yogurt preserves the complexion and bleaches away freckles.

Fresh, homemade sweet butter, with jam and bread or crackers, isn't a treat confined to farmers; anyone can make the dairy products pictured here. From left to right, front row, sweet butter and paraffin-coated, homemade hard cheese; back row, cream cheese made from yogurt, sour cream and cottage cheese.

1: An electric heating pad acts as an improvised yogurtmaker. Set at low heat, the pad has yogurt containers nestled into it and secured by the electric cord. To develop yogurt culture requires low, steady warmth. Any improvisation that can supply this warmth will do.

Rich in Nutrients

The rationale for these beliefs can be explained by yogurt's high protein, calcium, and lactic-acid content, which are beneficial to the skin. While yogurt's beneficial values do remain heartily controversial, it nevertheless is a very popular food. According to recent Department of Agriculture figures, Americans annually consume 25 million dollars' worth of yogurt.

Basic Yogurt is easy to make and is the basis for the dessert, salad dressing, soup, and cream cheese for which recipes are given on the opposite page. The bacteria are sensitive to temperature changes and the food they feed on. For best results, use fresh milk and fresh commercial yogurt as a starter. Aged yogurt used as a starter is less dependable.

Incubating Yogurt

First, plan how to keep the milk mixture warm enough for the culture to develop—between 105 and 112F—for 3 to 5 hours. Yogurtmaking appliances with temperature controls can be used, but you don't need one. An incubator can be easily improvised. You can nestle the yogurt jar in an electric heating pad, at the lowest setting, for 3 hours. Or place yogurt in a casserole; cover, and set in a pan of warm water on a radiator or in the oven at the lowest temperature for 3 to 5 hours. Or use a Balkan method: Pour warm yogurt mixture into a casserole; cover; wrap with a blanket, and leave in a warm room overnight. By morning the yogurt will be thick and ready for chilling.

Basic Yogurt

1 quart fresh milk	1 tablespoon plain, unflavored
2 tablespoons powdered milk	commercial yogurt

Combine fresh milk and powdered milk in a heavy, stainless-steel or enamel pot. Over low heat and stirring constantly, bring slowly to boiling point. Pour mixture into a bowl to cool to about 80 to 85F. Blend ½ cup of the warm milk with the yogurt until mixture is smooth. Then add this mixture to the bowl of remaining warm milk. Pour into a canning or freezer jar; cover, and keep warm, using one of the incubating methods described above. Incubate 3 to 5 hours—or overnight if you use blanket insulation. When the mixture is the consistency of thick cream, refrigerate it to chill before serving.

Makes four 8-ounce servings.

2: Pouring yogurt through a funnel helps avoid spills when containers have narrow necks. Use any clean bottle with a neck wide enough for a spoon to be used for scooping out yogurt after it has set. The bottle should be equipped with a cap.

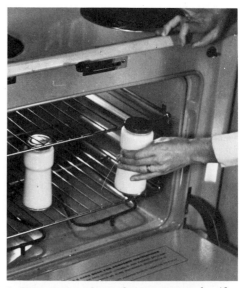

3: Your oven can be used as a yogurt-maker if it will hold a temperature setting of 105 to 112F steadily for several hours. If the oven heat goes above 115F, it may kill the bacteria whose actions make the yogurt ferment.

Fresh-Fruit Yogurt

1 quart fresh milk	1 tablespoon plain, unflavored
2 tablespoons powdered milk	commercial yogurt
½ cup fresh fruit or berries	Honey to taste

Scald fresh and powdered milk and cool to 110F. Incubate as directed for Basic Yogurt, and then mix in remaining ingredients. Refrigerate to chill before serving.

Makes four 9-ounce servings.

Yogurt Salad Dressing

1 cup Basic Yogurt	1 clove garlic, minced
⅓ cup apple-cider vinegar	½ cup chopped celery leaves
1 medium onion, minced	¼ cup chopped parsley leaves
⅔ cup safflower oil	

Blend all ingredients in an electric blender until smooth.

Makes 2½ cups.

Yogurt Tomato Soup

4 cups tomato juice	Pinch tarragon, preferably fresh
2 cups Basic Yogurt	Lemon twists (optional)

Blend tomato juice, yogurt, and tarragon in an electric blender until smooth. Serve cold. Garnish each serving with a twist of lemon, if desired.

Makes 6 servings.

Yogurt Cream Cheese

2 cups Basic Yogurt	Minced chives, green onions, herbs,
1 pinch sea salt	or savory seeds to taste; or
	fresh-fruit slices (optional)

Pour surface whey from yogurt. Mix in sea salt, and put yogurt into a bag made of three 12-by-18-inch layers of cheesecloth. Hang bag over sink, and let drain overnight, or until yogurt is consistency of cream cheese. Refrigerate. If desired, add one of optional flavorings before serving as a spread. For a sweet flavor, blend or serve with fresh-fruit slices. For a sharper cheese, use yogurt several days old.

Makes 2 cups.

4: Incubator for sour cream is improvised from potful of warm water and thick, warm blanket. Place container of buttermilk and fresh cream mixture in the warm water, and set pot on several thicknesses of the blanket. Wrap the rest of the blanket around pot and container, and leave overnight to incubate.

Making Sour Cream

Now that you have made several fermented dishes, you might like to try sour cream, which also depends on fermentation but uses a buttermilk culture instead of yogurt bacteria. Try sweetened sour cream with fresh fruits and fruit salad: Into 1 cup of sour cream stir 1 tablespoon of granulated sugar. Plain sour cream (2 cups) mixed with 1 small garlic clove, minced, makes a delicious dip for potato chips.

Sour Cream

1 pint fresh dairy heavy cream	5 teaspoons commercial cultured
	buttermilk

Thoroughly mix the cream and the buttermilk. (Shake buttermilk container well before measuring.) Pour mixture into a container that allows an inch or two of space at the top. Cover tightly, and shake thoroughly. Let stand in a warm place (70 to 85F) for 24 hours. Or improvise an incubator, as in photograph 4. Refrigerate. Serve cold.

Makes 1 pint.

Kitchen Favorites and Celebrations
Cheeses

There are many legends about the discovery of cheesemaking, most of them with elements in common: Someone sets out on horseback on a journey, taking along some milk in a pouch made from a calf's stomach. After some time, the traveler discovers that the milk has turned into a palatable sour curd.

Rennin, an enzyme from the lining of a calf's stomach, converts milk into curds and whey and is used almost universally in cheesemaking. The chief milk protein, casein, is curdled, or coagulated, by the enzyme action of rennet or pepsin, or by lactic acid produced by bacterial action, or by a combination of these.

Cheese is made from the milk of various animals, including cow, sheep, goat, buffalo, camel, ass, mare, llama, reindeer, yak, and zebu. As with yogurt, the flavor and consistency of cheese are determined by the type of milk and the conditions under which it is converted. And like wine, cheese has countless varieties. Basically, it is either soft or hard. Soft cheeses generally contain more moisture than hard cheeses. The homemaker can easily make soft cheeses, many of which have a cottage-cheese base. The recipe on the opposite page is a good takeoff point.

Making Cottage Cheese
Soft cheeses such as cottage cheese can be made with rennet, yogurt, or cultured buttermilk as a starter. The recipe opposite uses rennet. This can

Before there were dairy trucks, milk vendors dispensed their product in city streets, from pails, as shown in this sketch of a milkman of the 1820s.

5: Cheesecloth bag twisted at the top serves as a press to force out watery, sour whey after the rennet-set milk curds have been heated.

6: Shifting curds around by lifting the corners of the cheesecloth after whey has been removed loosens them so water can rinse through the curds in next step.

7: Loosened curds in their cheesecloth bag are dipped in cold water and then drained as shown here. The cheesecloth around them is not squeezed.

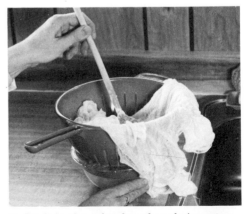

8: Back in the colander after their water bath, the curds are gently worked with a wooden spoon to loosen and lighten the mass. Cottage cheese is now ready to eat.

be purchased as junket rennet tablets, from Salada Foods, Inc., 399 Washington Street, Woburn, Mass. 01801, or as Hansen's cheese rennet tablets, from C. Hansen's Laboratories, 9015 West Maple Street, Milwaukee, Wis. 53214. A grocery store in your area may stock junket tablets; some pharmacies sell Hansen's; but both are usually difficult to obtain except from the manufacturers.

Coeur a la Creme—Heart of Cream—is shown with the heart-shape wicker basket traditionally used to drain and mold this classic French dessert.

Basic Cottage Cheese

1/6 Hansen's cheese rennet tablet, or
   2 junket rennet tablets
1/4 cup cold water

2 quarts skim milk
1/8 cup commercial cultured buttermilk

Dissolve the tablet in the cold water. Combine skim milk and buttermilk. Heat milk mixture to 70F. Add rennet solution, and stir well. Cover with a towel, and let stand at room temperature 12 to 18 hours, or until a smooth curd forms. With a long knife, cut the curd into ½-inch pieces. Slowly heat curds, in a double-boiler top over hot water, until temperature reaches 110F. Keep at this temperature 20 to 30 minutes, stirring about every 5 minutes so curds heat uniformly. When curds are firm, pour into a colander lined with cheesecloth, and let the whey drain off. Shift curds around by gently lifting the corners of the cloth. After whey has drained off, draw corners of cloth together, and immerse for about 2 seconds in cold water. Work curds with a wooden spoon to free them of any excess whey. Stir; chill.

Makes 8 servings

A Cheese-Based Dessert

A delicious and simple dessert called Coeur a la Creme—Heart of Cream—can be made with Yogurt Cream Cheese, page 449, or Basic Cottage Cheese, above. Any fresh fruit may be used to garnish it. It is molded in a heart-shape basket.

Coeur a la Creme

4 cups homemade cream cheese or
   cottage cheese
1 cup Basic Yogurt

2 tablespoons granulated sugar
1 pint fresh berries, sliced
Granulated sugar to taste

Stir cheese, at room temperature, with yogurt and 2 tablespoons sugar until smooth. Line heart-shape basket with cheesecloth; set on soup plate. Pack mixture into basket; drain and chill several hours, or overnight. To serve, unmold; garnish with berries; sprinkle with sugar to taste.

Makes 8 servings.

Cottage-Cheese Dip

2 cups homemade cottage cheese
1 teaspoon celery seeds
1 teaspoon dill seeds
1 teaspoon caraway seeds

1 teaspoon minced parsley
1 teaspoon minced chives
Pinch paprika

Blend cottage cheese with celery, dill, and caraway seeds. Add parsley and chives. Chill for several hours. Before serving, sprinkle lightly with paprika. Serve with crackers or bread rounds.

Makes 2 cups.

Making Hard Cheese

Hard cheeses usually travel better and last longer than soft cheeses, but they are more complex and time-consuming to make. Most people, except the adventurous, will not bother with home preparation. But if you would like to try making hard cheese, the recipe on page 452 is a basic one. When you are making hard cheese, remember that Marco Polo brought cheese similar to this one from the Orient to Europe. In the days before refrigeration and rapid transportation, it was one of the staple foods for long-distance travelers, because it was nutritive, kept well, and was easily carried.

9: Test curd for hard cheese to see if it is firm enough. If curd slides down your finger instead of breaking cleanly over it, let curd set longer.

10: Cut curds with a long-bladed knife. Note that the pieces of curd here are quite small, about ⅜ inch in size. As you cut, avoid crushing the curds.

11: Place curds in the center of a double layer of cheesecloth; then pull cloth corners together to form a cradle, and roll curds in it gently.

Basic Process for Hard Cheese

The basic process for making hard cheese is similar to that for soft cheese, but hard cheeses are usually made in large batches because they keep well and are aged several weeks before use. The recipe below makes a single 6-pound cheese, or six 1-pound cheeses. By doubling proportions, you can make a cheese twice the size. John Leland, a Cheshire, Mass., cheesemaker, presented President Jefferson with a cheese weighing 1,235 pounds—which is to say you can make hard cheese in very large sizes.

If you plan to make hard cheese often, you will want to have a cheese press. A simple one for small cheeses can be constructed from two 8-by-12-inch pieces of ¾-inch board, sanded. Join them with two 1-inch dowels, one centered through each end. With the lump of fresh cheese on the lower board, press the top board down, flattening the cheese evenly as you press out the remaining whey. As a substitute, set the cheese on a large, clean plate; set another plate on top, and weight—with an iron, for instance.

Hard cheese is coated with paraffin or oil before its aging period.

Basic Hard Cheese

2 gallons fresh milk (preferably raw)	1 cup cold water
¾ Hansen's cheese rennet tablet, or 8 junket rennet tablets	2 tablespoons sea salt

Let 1 gallon of the milk ripen overnight in a cool place (50 to 60F). The following morning, add the other gallon. In a large, enamel or stainless-steel pot, warm the milk to 86F. Add tablet to the cold water, and stir until dissolved. Set pot in a larger vessel of warm water (88 to 90F), away from drafts. Add rennet solution, and stir thoroughly. Let stand undisturbed until a firm curd forms—about 30 to 45 minutes. Test firmness by carefully putting a finger into the curd at an angle and lifting it. If curd breaks cleanly over your finger, it is ready to cut. If not, let it set 15 to 20 minutes longer.

Remove pot from larger vessel, and cut curd into ⅜-inch cubes. Use a knife with a blade long enough to cut through to bottom of pot without the handle's touching the curd. Stir curd cubes carefully but thoroughly with wooden spoon about 15 minutes; use long, slow movements so curds are not crushed. Place pot in a larger pot with water (creating a double-boiler effect), and heat slowly, raising curds' temperature about 1½ degrees every 5 minutes until it reaches 102F. Stir with a wooden spoon to keep curds from sticking together. Remove from heat when curds start to hold their shape and readily fall apart when held, but not squeezed, together.

Stir every 5 minutes for about 1 hour (that's right!) to keep curds from sticking. Leave them in the whey until the mass becomes so firm that a handful of pieces, pressed together, will shake apart easily. Put the curds on a double layer of 3-foot-square cheesecloth, and pull corners of cloth together. Swing gently, letting curds roll back and forth so whey drains without squeezing. Sprinkle curds with half of sea salt, and mix well with wooden spoon. Sprinkle on remaining sea salt, and mix in by hand.

Tie cheesecloth so curds form a ball; hang up, and let whey drip for 45 minutes. Remove cheesecloth; fold it into a rectangular bandage, 3 inches by 3 feet, and wrap tightly around the ball. With your hands, press down on ball until top and bottom are flat. Put three or four layers of cheesecloth under and over the cheese. Place in press; adjust pieces of wood; put a heavy object on the press; leave overnight. Turn; press overnight again.

Remove cheese from the press, and remove cheesecloth wrapping. Let stand in a warm room (70 to 75F) for 6 hours while rind forms and dries out. Then coat with hot, melted paraffin. Holding cheese with tongs, dip one half and then the other. Or paint on paraffin with a basting brush. An alternate to paraffin coating is rubbing vegetable oil into the cheese. Ripen in a cool place (50 to 65F) 3 to 4 weeks; turn two or three times a week.

Makes about one pound of cheese.

Kitchen Favorites and Celebrations
Churning

Churning or agitating is the process that makes fat globules in milk unite—the end product is butter. The process dates back to about 2000 B.C., when churning was achieved by filling skin pouches with milk and throwing them back and forth or letting them swing over the backs of trotting horses. The butter made then was used most often as an ointment for the bath, a medicine or an illuminating oil.

As butter became a staple food, hand churns for the dairy were devised—rotating, swinging, or rocking barrels or boxes and cylindrical vessels equipped with plungers or dashers. Today, butter is made with electric churns. Churning time depends on the composition of the butterfat; the temperature, acidity, and richness of the cream; the speed and motion of the churn; and the size of the fat globules.

Butter's natural color, which ranges from pale yellow to deep gold, is derived from the carotene in the fodder the milk-giving animal—the cow or some other animal—has eaten. In the United States, cream from cow's milk is generally used in making butter; but in other countries, cream from the milk of goats, sheep, and mares is converted into butter.

All butter, when it is freshly made, is sweet. Salt is added to butter as a preservative and for flavor. You can easily make your own fresh, sweet butter using an electric mixer. When heavy cream is whipped long enough, it is transformed into little round, yellow globules of fat swimming in a bowl of whey. When it is beaten for another minute or so, the grainy, yellow lumps join together to form a ball of butter.

You can follow the recipe below to make a variety of flavored butters. Just beat in honey or salt to taste, or add herbs, spices, or other flavorings.

Flavored Butter

½ pint heavy cream   ½ to 1 teaspoon salt, herbs,
                                   spices, or other flavorings

In a medium bowl whip cream with an electric mixer at medium speed until butter separates from whey. Pour off whey; beat in flavoring.
Makes ¼ pound.

Making Fresh Mayonnaise
A churning process with a different principle behind it produces a delicious fresh mayonnaise. By beating mustard into the yolks of eggs, along with a bit of salt and a little vinegar or lemon juice, you create a chemical change that allows the yolks to absorb quantities of oil, rather as rice absorbs water when it is boiled. The result is a creamy, golden mayonnaise with a unique flavor. It is an excellent dressing for meat salads, cold vegetables, and potato salad. Sweetened with 1 teaspoon granulated sugar and mixed half and half with whipped cream, it is delicious with jellied salad rings.

Mayonnaise

1 teaspoon salt   2 tablespoons vinegar or lemon juice
½ teaspoon dry mustard   1½ cups salad oil
2 egg yolks   Pinch cayenne

In a medium bowl, mix salt, mustard, egg yolks, and 1 teaspoon vinegar. With electric mixer at high speed, beat in ¼ of the oil, a few dribbles at a time. Add the remaining vinegar and the cayenne. Slowly beat in the remaining oil. Keep refrigerated.
Makes 1¾ cups.
For related projects and crafts see "Breads," "Brewing," "Colonial Crafts," "Herbs," "Winemaking."

12: Adding egg yolks to salt and mustard is first step in making fresh mayonnaise. Stir mixture with a wooden spoon until the ingredients form a smooth paste. Then stir in 1 teaspoon of the vinegar.

13: With electric mixer at high speed, beat the egg mixture while dribbling in ¼ of the oil, a few drops at a time. Next, beat in remaining vinegar; then slowly dribble in remaining oil.

14: Garnish with a few tarragon leaves, and the finished mayonnaise is ready to be served. It has a rich golden color and a thick, creamy texture and holds its shape like whipped cream.

CHRISTMAS CELEBRATIONS
All through the House

Elvin McDonald is garden editor and senior editor of House Beautiful *magazine and a popular garden lecturer and writer. He has been gardening all his life and, at the age of 12, founded the American Gloxinia Society. His many publications include* The World Book of House Plants, Gardening under Lights, *and the 16-volume* Good Housekeeping Illustrated Encyclopedia of Gardening, *for which he was executive editor.*

Christmas is that warm and wonderful time of year when we renew ties with old friends and exchange sentiments of good will. True to this ideal, we give and receive gifts on the big day, but I think the real enjoyment of Christmas lies in its preparation. This can be a time of genuine family togetherness and group effort. Instead of the usual last-minute pressure of buying gifts and manufactured decorations, why not return to the Christmas of Colonial times—strings of cranberry and popcorn, handcrafted ornaments, and wreaths of fresh pine? With a little effort and planning, you can bring the warmth of an authentically traditional Christmas into your home.

Many of our Christmas traditions—the use of evergreens included—originated as part of ancient holiday rituals. The Celts believed that evergreens placed over the entrances to their homes had the power to ward off evil spirits, and they placed sprigs of holly and mistletoe indoors as symbols of eternal life. The Romans raised an evergreen bough to celebrate the winter solstice. At the same time of year, they celebrated the feast of Saturn, and the New Year that followed, with banquets, exchanges of gifts, and the use of decorative greenery and torches.

The custom of bringing an evergreen tree indoors originated in the fifteenth century in western Germany, where forests of fir trees abounded. The decorated Christmas tree became popular around 1500 in the area of the upper Rhine River. It was adorned with paper ornaments and edible decorations, such as apples and sugar, and in Scandinavia and other parts of northern Europe, trees are still decorated in this manner. In Colonial America, trimmings included various kinds of fruit, strings of popcorn and cranberries, ribbons, polished nuts, and colored papers.

Living Christmas Trees

I prefer a living tree for Christmas. Balled and burlaped, it can later be planted in your yard or potted for your apartment terrace. Best for in-ground planting, in areas where needled evergreens prosper, are firs, pines, spruces, and upright yews *(Taxus capitata)*. For container planting, choose a pine or upright yew. Hemlocks are not likely to survive a stay indoors.

Buy from a reliable nursery. Test a tree's health by pulling its needles; if they come off easily, the tree is too dry. Avoid trees with branch yellowing, especially near the trunks. If you live in northern areas, it's a good idea to dig the planting hole in the fall before the ground freezes. Fill the hole with straw, or cover with a tarpaulin. Later, drag the heavy root ball on the tarp for easy moving. When you bring the tree home, store it outdoors with roots wrapped in a blanket. Indoors, don't stand the tree near

In the inset photograph are colorful ribbons and candy wreaths; instructions are on page 464. In the large photograph are handcrafted tree ornaments. Instructions for the painted balls and the tasseled-fringe ball, far right, are on page 459.

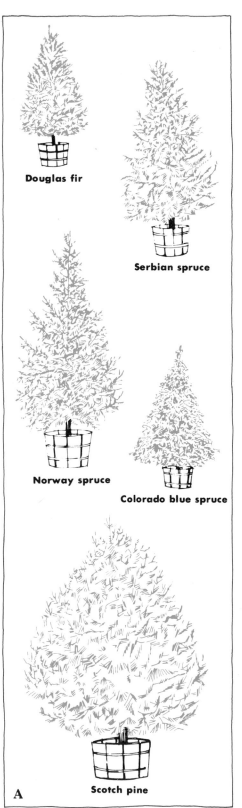

Figure A: All of these Christmas-tree favorites are available live at your nursery. Small trees (5 feet and under) are easiest to handle and have the best chance for survival. Trees are shown here planted in wooden planters, as they would be on a patio or apartment terrace.

Douglas fir

Serbian spruce

Norway spruce

Colorado blue spruce

Scotch pine

A

a fireplace or other heat sources. To keep the earth surrounding the roots moist, place the tree in a tub, dishpan, or child's flying saucer, with an inch or two of water in it at all times. Wedge some kindling wood under edges of the root ball to hold the tree securely upright. If your nurseryman hasn't already done so, spray the tree with an antidesiccant (see figure B, opposite). This is a transparent-plastic coating that will help keep the needles green and moisture filled.

Cut Christmas Trees

If you prefer a cut Christmas tree, the Forest Service of the United States Department of Agriculture makes these recommendations for its handling:

☐ Select a fresh, green tree with resilient needles and strong scent.

☐ Saw off the butt end of the tree (see figure C, opposite).

☐ Keep the butt end standing in a container of water during the entire time the tree is indoors.

☐ Be sure the tree is well supported and is away from fireplaces, radiators, television sets, and other sources of heat.

☐ Never use lighted candles or other open flames on or near the tree.

1: Lights go on tree first. Begin at top, and wind around and down. Before hanging, plug in to check for loose or dead bulbs.

2: Push bead up to tighten wires around branch. These small lights use little electricity and do not overwhelm the other ornaments.

3: After covering tree, plug in lights; adjust spacing; then secure each light by looping wire around branch as shown.

Garlands of popcorn and cranberries, folded-paper stars, patchwork balls, candy, fruit, and real carnations make this a sumptuous, yet traditional, Christmas tree.

Figure B: To protect a live tree against dryness, spray with antidesiccant from a garden store. Keep balled roots moist in tub or resting on child's flying saucer.

Figure C: For cut tree, saw off trunk at least an inch above original cut. Position in a sturdy stand according to directions; add water every day or two.

□ Never use worn, frayed wires. Check lights and connections.
□ Don't use combustible decorations or flammable reflectors for lights.
□ Avoid overloading electric circuits. Don't leave accumulations of wrapping paper or electrical toys under the tree.

You can prolong the life of your cut Christmas tree by following this procedure: To one gallon of boiling water add four teaspoons of chlorinated bleach, four tablespoons of micronized iron (available at garden centers under various trade names), and two cups of corn syrup. Place the freshly sawed trunk in this solution, and let it stand there two or three hours. Also put this solution in the tree-holder well; add warm water as needed.

To make your cut tree more fire-resistant, add nine ounces of borax and four ounces of boric-acid crystals or powder to one gallon of warm water. Mix, and apply the solution to the tree with a mist-type sprayer.

Designs and Decorations
Patchwork Christmas balls ¢ ⊠ 👶 🎨

These patchwork Christmas-tree balls are easy to make and so lightweight that even the largest will not make the branches of your tree sag.

To make them, you will need as many foam balls as you wish, in various sizes (available at hobby shops); medium-weight florist's wire (buy two or three spools at your garden center, since it is essential for many of the projects on these pages); tin snips to cut the wire (or you can use side-cutting pliers or old scissors); ribbons or scraps of cloth patterned in assorted checks, stripes, and polka dots; sharp scissors; enough ribbon to make a few squares and a bow for each ball; and a container of white glue.

Follow this procedure: Cut a piece of florist's wire as long as the foam ball's diameter plus 7 inches for securing and hanging. Push it through the center of the ball. Form a loop at one end (see photograph 6), for hanging the ball. Leave about an inch of excess wire at the other end. Bend this, and push the end back into the foam to secure the wire. Cut the ribbons or cloth scraps into roughly 1-inch squares. Apply glue to the backs, and press squares onto the ball. Tie a ribbon bow around the base of the wire loop.

From Indiana, Stephen Barany is a successful New York florist and designer. His Christmas creations combine Old World charm with contemporary ingenuity.

4: Here are glue, fabric scraps, ribbon, and foam ball needed to make a patchwork ornament. It will be most attractive if you use fabrics of different patterns but of the same color or color combination.

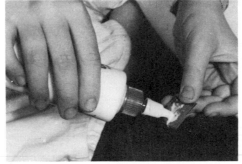

5: Apply glue, and then smear it over back of square with your finger. Press and smooth the square onto the foam ball.

6: Apply squares at random, and overlap slightly. Use some squares cut from the ribbon for the bow (see photograph below).

This tree ornament recalls the charm and folksiness of a patchwork quilt. It is easy to make, something the whole family, including the children, can do.

Designs and Decorations
Handmade Christmas balls ¢ ⌧ 👫 🧵

To make the tasseled-fringe ornament on the right in the color photograph on page 455, you will need a 6-inch foam ball, a small, round mirror, white glue, scissors, a scrap of felt, 1 yard of gold braid, straight pins, 1 yard of tasseled fringe, a garland of gold and a garland of pink tiny balls, bead-headed pins, large sequins, and florist's wire for hanging.

Glue and press mirror onto ball to flatten form. Cut a 2-inch diameter circle of felt, and glue to side of ball directly opposite mirror. Wrap and pin inch-wide strip of gold braid around mirror (photograph 7). Wrap and pin three rows of fringe around ball center. Thread bead-headed pins with gold garland balls in twos, and position pins to form circle around center of ball at fringe. Pin gold braid so it covers edge of felt and area between felt and fringe (photograph 8). Thread bead-headed pins with single pink ball and sequin, and position pins to form circle at outer edge of gold braid around mirror. Thread bead-headed pins with one gold ball; pin around mirror edge.

To make one of the painted balls in the photograph on page 455, you will need a new or an old glass or plastic ball, a can of artist's canvas primer (sold at art-supply stores), two or three artist's paintbrushes, a felt marker, tubes of acrylic paint in various colors, and a spray can of clear lacquer.

Pull off ball's cap and hanger. Paint with primer (photograph 9), and let dry. Draw design with marker (photograph 10), and paint with acrylic paint (photograph 11). Spray with lacquer. Replace cap and hanger.

Maria Lench, an artist, majored in art at San Diego State College and the University of Colorado. Her creative designs include these unusual and attractive Christmas ornaments.

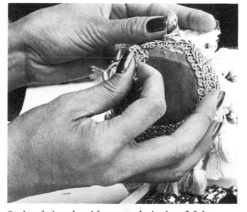

7: Wrap gold braid around mirror. As you pin braid down, overlap edges slightly so white foam will not show through.

8: Applying braid around circle of felt. Overlap felt slightly. When finished, pierce ball with wire for hanging.

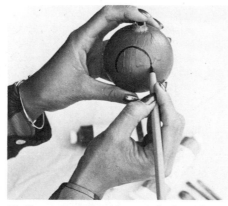

9: For painted ornament, prime the ball with artist's canvas primer (gesso). Your overlay design of acrylic paint will adhere permanently to this base coat.

10: For a guideline, draw a design of your choosing with a felt-tip marking pen. Any mistakes in design execution can later be corrected by covering with acrylic paint.

11: Use bright colors to fill in design. Experiment with geometric shapes. Allow paint to dry thoroughly, and spray the ball with clear lacquer.

Designs and Decorations
Natural and paper trims $ ◫ ⁂ ⁂

On the tree pictured in color on page 457, I used pink and red carnations, cranberry and cranberry-popcorn garlands, apples, pears, and crab apples, ribbon candy, candy kisses, and large gumdrops. To decorate your tree this way, you will need, in addition to the natural materials, florist's wire and some old scissors or side-cutting pliers to cut it; a spool of thread and a sewing needle (a needle and length of thread for each member of the family will make stringing popcorn and cranberries a pleasant group activity); and a plastic watering tube or vial (photograph 12) for each of your fresh flowers. These tubes are sold at florist's shops.

Candy
The reflective quality of the foil wrapping on candy kisses makes them ideal tree decorations. Thread seven or eight of them on some florist's wire; twist ends of wire together, forming a circle. If you work gently, kisses will not break apart. Attach a wire loop for hanging the ring of kisses.

Gumdrops (see color photograph, left) and ribbon candy (see photograph of tree, page 458) also make colorful ornaments. Thread three or four gumdrops, through the bottom and out the top, on a length of florist's wire. Bend the wire at the bottom of the gumdrop column to secure it. Form a loop with the wire at the top to hang the column on your tree. For the ribbon candy, twist one end of a short length of wire around one of the end candy loops, and form a loop with the other end of the wire to hang candy vertically on the tree.

Cranberry and Popcorn Garlands
Of all the kinds of garlands used for Christmas trees, I think those made of strung popcorn and cranberries are the most attractive. Buy two or three boxes of cranberries. Make a large bowl or two of popcorn at least two weeks before you intend to string it, so it has plenty of time to soften. Leave the popcorn in the kitchen; the steam from cooking will ensure its softness. Also, be sure to use the old-fashioned kind of popcorn, not the kind sold as extra crisp.

String two types of garland—one solely of cranberries and the other alternating two pieces of popcorn with two cranberries. Use no more than a 4-foot length of double thread at a time; longer thread is unwieldy. Thread the needle, and knot the ends of the thread with a double knot. Pierce each cranberry and piece of popcorn with the needle, and slide it onto the thread. Don't fill the entire thread; leave 6 inches between the needle and the last berry or piece of popcorn. Cut this thread from the needle, and tie it to one of the tree's uppermost branches. Wind the garland down and around the tree, draping it as you go. Start the second string where the first one ends, and continue in the same manner with more garlands until you reach the bottom of the tree.

Fruit and Flowers
Apples, pears, and crab apples are fine tree decorations and can be secured easily to the tree. Simply pierce them through the length of their cores with florist's wire, bend the wire's bottom end, and push it into the fruit. Wind the top end of the wire around one of the larger branches or close to the tree trunk on a smaller branch.

You can decorate your tree with whatever fresh flowers you wish, as long as you provide watering tubes (see photograph 12) for all of them and put the flowers into the tubes before you attach them to the tree. The flowers will last from Christmas Eve to New Year's Day if the tubes are kept filled with water. Secure a tube to the tree by placing it upright against a branch, with the flower facing out, and wrapping tube and branch with florist's wire (or you can use florist's tape). Don't cover the tube's rubber stopper.

Natural and edible items make charming decorations for your tree. This detail shows gumdrops, candy canes, apples, a pear, cranberry garland, and a carnation. Small, brightly colored toys, such as the red-and-white drum shown, also are appropriate ornaments.

12: To keep flower fresh, cut stem short, and slide into a water-filled tube. Check water level daily; refill as needed.

Paper star. A sheet of paper 7 by 7 inches makes a star 6½ by 7 inches. Use any size paper, as long as it is square. For the best-looking star, use foil wrapping paper that is white on one side. Begin by folding paper in half from top to bottom. Open, and fold in half from left to right. Open; turn over, and follow photographs.

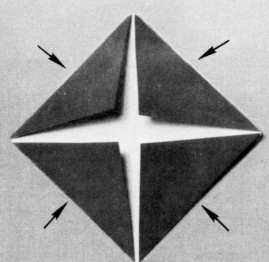

STEP I
Fold corner to point where two folds cross.

STEP II
Fold in all corners in same manner.

STEP III
Fold in half, left to right, and open.

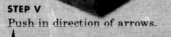

STEP IV
Fold in half, top to bottom. Grasp at
✳ points with thumbs and forefingers.

STEP V
Push in direction of arrows.

STEP VI
Join flaps in pairs,
and press flat.

STEP VII
Fold in upper side flaps.

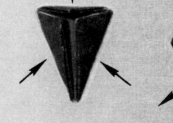

STEP VIII
Turn over, and fold in side flaps; fold
top flap down.

STEP IX
Open three flaps
folded in step **VIII**; then
insert finger underneath
upper flap at ✳ point.

STEP X
Gently pull up uppermost
flap from bottom until
elongated diamond is formed.

STEP XI
Press flat on hard surface.

STEP XII
Turn over; repeat steps
VII-X, and fold down
top flap.

STEP XIII
Turn over, and
fold down top flap as
in step **XII**.

STEP XIV
Grasp inner flaps at ✳ points, and pull
apart in direction of arrows until...

STEP XV
Completed star
snaps into shape.

Paper Folding and Cutting
Christmas gift wraps

This Christmas, be clever and creative in your gift wrapping. At left are some ideas, and below are basic instructions for wrapping a gift box.

Interesting package trimmings that hint at what might be inside are easy to improvise. Top, glued-on scoop and raw rice. Bottom, wooden utensils and basket.

Fun wraps for children include, left, fabric wrapping with small stuffed animal taped on and, right, the Sunday comics, for color and comedy no child can resist.

Toy soldiers stand guard over a foil-wrapped package, decorated with a small plastic box and paper flowers.

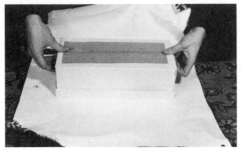

13: Place box, lid down, on paper. Center it, and be sure paper is large enough to wrap around box and overlap 1 inch.

15: Bring up the other side of the paper, and overlap the first. Fold the edge under, and tape it to the paper beneath.

17: Fold down the top paper flap, and tape it. Be sure sides of paper under flap are smoothed closely against box.

19: For something different in ribbon trimming, wrap a length of wide ribbon around box, and tape two ends together.

14: Bring one side of the paper up and over; fold the edge under for neatness, and tape to the box along the fold.

16: Push in sides of end paper, squaring it neatly against box. End-paper length should be slightly less than box depth.

18: Fold over the edge of the bottom flap. Then fold the flap against the box, and tape it securely along its edge.

20: Over the wide ribbon, wrap a narrow one of coordinating or contrasting color, and tape two ends together.

Greenery and Growing Things
Wheat-and-flower wreath $$ ▯ ⅄ ⚱

Using wheat or straw trimmed with dried flowers and an occasional edible, such as cookies and small cakes, is a centuries-old Christmas tradition in the Slavic countries of eastern Europe. These natural materials—used to make the wreath shown here and the tree in the color photograph on page 466—will add a pleasant rustic and folk-oriented touch to your Christmas.

To make the wreath shown in the color photograph, right, you will need a 20-inch-diameter foam wreath form; six pounds of dried wheat stalks (there are about 100 to a pound); two boxes (150 to a box) of steel flower picks (see photograph 21); a pair of pliers; three dozen U-shape florist's pins; large and small silk poppies and dried daisies, poppy seed pods, buttercups, and delphiniums. Poppies are one of the few flowers that cannot be dried. Purchase the others already dried, or you can use flowers you have dried (see the entry "Dried Flowers," in Volume Five). All these materials are available at your florist's, or he can get them for you at a flower market. For an optional trimming, purchase a dozen pastry-type cookies at your bakery. Follow this step-by-step procedure to make the wheat-and-flower wreath:

Cut the tops of all the wheat stalks to 9-inch lengths.

Bunch three or four stalks together, and secure them with a steel flower pick (see photograph 21). Use pliers to bend the small tabs of the pick around the wheat stalks.

Attach the stalks to the wreath form by inserting the pick into the foam at a sharp angle, so the stalks lie almost flat (see photograph 22). Cover the entire form, including the sides, this way. Do not cover the back. Make sure all the stalks lean in the same direction around the wreath.

Insert U-shape pins wherever they are needed (photograph 23).

Attach steel picks to all the dried or silk flowers you are using, and push the picks through the wheat stalks and into the foam. Fewer picks will be required if you gather three or four flowers into bunches and use one pick for each bunch.

Attach a pick to each poppy seed pod, and insert it into the foam.

If you wish, you can add cookies to the trimmings. Small, decorative, pastry-type cookies are appropriate for this kind of wreath. Carefully pierce the cookies with florist's wire; bend the wire close to the cookie to hold it, and hook the other end of the wire into the foam.

The tree on page 466 is made the same way as the wreath, but on a 35-inch-high foam Christmas-tree form. Again, the wheat stalks are inserted at a sharp angle. In imitation of the branches of a real tree, they should lie almost flat, with their tops downward. Trim with flowers and cookies (optional) in the same manner as the wreath. Tiny wooden toys or figures, if you have some, are also appropriate for this kind of tree.

Maria Wizmur was born on the border of Poland and Russia and was raised in Hungary. Her love of beauty, primarily in flowers, prompted her to become a floral designer. She sells her work at Les Fleurs Gallery in Woodbury, N.Y.

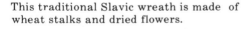
This traditional Slavic wreath is made of wheat stalks and dried flowers.

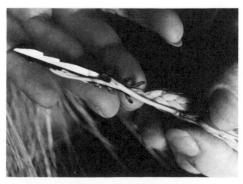

21: Wheat stalks in steel flower pick. Press the small clamps firmly around the stalks with pliers. Teeth on the pick keep it securely in the foam.

22: Insert the picks, with the stalks attached, into the foam at a sharp angle. Place them close to one another, and overlap stalks generously, as shown.

23: Inserting a U-shape pin. After you have covered the form, use pins to gather and hold any stray stalks and generally shape and tidy the wreath.

Designs and Decorations
Candy wreaths

A child's fantasy of Candyland could not conjure up anything more sumptuous than a wreath generously covered with all kinds of candy. This little Christmas project is something children can do—if they are not overcome by the temptation to eat all the materials. With a little supervision, they can make the wreaths in the photograph below or create their own variations.

To make these wreaths, you will need three 10-inch-diameter foam wreath forms (available at a florist's or a craft store); two boxes of flat, wooden toothpicks (rounded ones tend to fall out of the foam); a pound each of gumdrops, ribbon candy, candy kisses, small marzipan candies shaped and colored like fruit, and three jars of soft candied cherries (all these are available in supermarkets); and ribbon for bows.

Break some toothpicks in half. Push a candy onto the end of a toothpick half, and insert the rest of the toothpick all the way into the foam. Break the ribbon candy into 1-inch pieces; secure these by placing two or three whole toothpicks topped with candied cherries into the foam around the ribbon candy. For each wreath, cover the entire form, except the space for a bow.

Jeannene McDonald works intently on her gumdrop wreath. She places gumdrops on the form as close together as possible.

Jeannene (center) and David and Holly Hunter display their wreaths. David's is of ribbon candy and cherries, and Holly's of marzipan, gumdrops, cherries, and kisses.

Greenery and Growing Things
Mantelpiece wreath

Preserve a tradition of Christmases past by fashioning a wreath of fresh greenery. You will need a wire coat hanger; two dozen 6- to 12-inch-long evergreen branches (you can cut them from a tree or shrub in your yard, or buy a taller Christmas tree than needed and use the lower branches); a spool of medium-weight florist's wire and a wire cutter (see materials listed on page 458); scissors; crab apples; and 2 yards of wide ribbon for a bow.

Figure D: Use florist's wire and wire hanger to make greenery wreath. Hanger need not be bent into perfect circle. Leave hook on hanger so wreath can be hung easily.

The hearth is a Christmas gathering place. Wreath instructions are given here. To make the stockings, see the entry "Granny Squares," in Volume Seven.

Bend coat hanger as shown in figure D. Bunch two or three branches; wind wire around their bases. Begin winding wire on coat-hanger frame (figure D, left). Place branch bunch on frame; wind wire around base of branches and frame (figure D, center). Try not to catch upper part of branches; they should be loose. Continue around frame (figure D, right). Make sure all branches lie in same direction. When hanger is covered, cut wire, and trim greens, if necessary, with scissors. Add crab apples, as pictured. Pierce each with wire, and twist wire around greens. To make the bow, see figure E.

Loop ribbon and, as if wringing a wash cloth, twist free end at point where loop ends meet.

Make eight loops, alternating from side to side and holding at central point. Twist each time, as in the previous step, and pin or wrap with wire at center to hold.

Tie a short length of ribbon around center; let ends hang free.

Figure E: Follow these steps to make a wreath bow. Use 2 yards of wide ribbon. Attach to wreath with wire.

Kitchen Favorites and Celebrations
Christmas buffet

A tree-trimming party the Sunday before Christmas is traditional. A simple buffet, with hot mulled wine (wassail bowl) and cold eggnog, hot mincemeat pie and rich fruit cake, makes feeding the decorators easy. Fruit cake and mince meat can be prepared weeks ahead. The recipes here make four large pies and four cakes—enough to feed tree trimmers and provide handsome gifts.

Mulled Wine with Cranberries

2 bottles, or ½ gallon, dry red wine
½ teaspoon ground mace
6 teaspoon honey
1 cup fresh cranberries, washed

1 cup brandy (optional)
4 cinnamon sticks
3 thin slices lemon
3 thin slices orange

In a 3-quart saucepan, heat the wine, mace, honey, and half the cranberries until almost boiling. Stir in brandy. Pour into 3- and 4-quart serving bowl. Float lemon and orange slices and remaining cranberries on top. Stir with cinnamon sticks; then float the sticks in the wine. Makes 16 to 20 servings.

Felt-covered table pinned with ribbons bears traditional treats: mulled wine fruit cake, mincemeat pie, eggnog. Wheat-tree directions are on page 463.

Eggnog

1 pint heavy cream	1 cup brandy (optional)
6 eggs	2 quarts cold, whole milk
1 teaspoon vanilla extract	Grated rind 1 orange
4 tablespoons sugar	⅛ teaspoon nutmeg
½ teaspoon ground mace	

Whip cream until stiff. Beat eggs, vanilla, sugar, mace, and brandy until thick. Stir in milk. Pour into a 4-quart serving bowl. Stir in whipped cream. Sprinkle with grated orange rind and nutmeg. Makes 16 servings.

Fruit Cake

1½ pounds shortening	1 pound each pitted dates, candied cherries, angelica
2 pounds sugar	
2 pounds pastry flour	3 pounds sultana raisins
1 teaspoon each allspice, cinnamon, baking soda	1 pound each chopped pecans, slivered blanched almonds
14 eggs	½ cup rum or brandy
1 teaspoon almond extract	½ pound each pecan halves, angelica squares, candied cherries.
4 pounds mixed, candied fruits	

In a very large salad bowl or 5-quart kettle, cream shortening with sugar. Into another bowl, sift flour with allspice, cinnamon, and soda. In another large bowl, beat eggs and almond extract until thick. Beat egg and flour mixtures alternately into shortening mixture. On floured board, chop candied fruits, dates, 1 pound cherries and angelica; mix with raisins. Chop 1 pound pecans coarsely. Mix fruits, chopped pecans, and almonds; beat into batter. Mix in rum. Turn into 4 greased, floured, 7- or 8-inch tube pans. Decorate with candied cherries, angelica squares, and pecan halves. Bake in preheated 275F oven 2 hours, or until straw inserted in centers comes out clean. Cool in pans on rack 2 or 3 hours. Turn out; wrap in cheesecloth rinsed in rum; seal with foil. Makes 4.

Mincemeat

¾ pound white beef suet	½ pound blanched almonds
¾ pound each currants, raisins, sultana raisins	1 ounce blanched bitter almonds
	⅛ teaspoon each cinnamon, mace, salt, white pepper
¾ pound peeled, chopped apple	
½ pound each chopped citron, candied orange peel, candied lemon peel	¾ cup brandy
	Grated rind 1 lemon
	Strained juice 1 lemon

Put suet through fine blade of chopper twice. In large bowl, combine suet with currants, raisins, and apple. Finely chop citron, peels, and almonds; add to suet mixture. Combine cinnamon, mace, salt, and pepper; add to suet mixture. Bake, in ovenproof dish, in preheated 300F oven 30 minutes. Remove from oven; stir in brandy, lemon rind and juice. Seal in a 4- or 5-quart crock or bowl. Will keep in refrigerator 2 weeks, or if frozen, indefinitely. Makes enough for 4 big pies.

Mincemeat Pie

Pastry dough for 2-crust; 9-inch pie
Cold milk
4 cups mincemeat

Fit bottom crust into 8- or 9-inch pie plate. Fill with mincemeat. Cover with top crust; slash, and brush with cold milk. Bake in preheated 350F oven 45 minutes. Makes 8 to 10 servings.

For other Christmas projects, see the entries, "Birthday Celebrations," "Confections and Comfits," "Dried Flowers," "Foam," "Granny Squares," "Greeting Cards," "Papercrafts," "Papier- and Cloth-Mache," "Pine-Cone Constructions," "Ribboncraft," and "Spool Toys."

CLAMBAKES
The Ultimate Cookout

North American Indians were having clambakes before the first settlers from Europe reached New England. The Indians cooked their clams, corn and other food, much as many New England clambakers have done, in pits about 2 feet deep lined with stones. First a fire was built on the stones to heat them, and damp seaweed was placed on the hot stones to produce steam. Then the food was placed on the seaweed and more seaweed was placed on the food. Cooking time using this traditional method was 8 to 10 hours, a tribute to the patience of the Indians and early settlers.

Another clambake cooking method involves digging a pit in the sand, burying a large barrel almost to the top in the pit, and adding a small amount of water to the barrel. Stones heated in a separate fire are then put in the barrel, followed by successive layers of seaweed and food until the barrel is full. A tarp is tied down over the barrel top, which is then covered with sand. Cooking time using this method is only a few hours, but it takes a long time to dig the pit and heat the stones.

The clambake technique popular today substitutes for the pit or barrel a sheet of steel about 4 by 8 feet, set on rock or cinder-block supports built 1½ to 2 feet above ground. A wood fire heats the steel sheet, and layers of seaweed and food are placed on the steel, and then covered with a tarp. Cooking takes about an hour and the setup can feed dozens of people easily, making it ideal for club, neighborhood or community groups. Dividing the costs of the structural ingredients over a large group also makes such clambakes more palatable financially. The edible ingredients (lobsters, clams, corn, potatoes, onions, chicken and hotdogs) will be costly enough today.

Formerly a florist, Bill Foster began organizing clambakes for friends and summer visitors in his York Harbor, Me. backyard more than 22 years ago. More recently Foster, and his wife Phoebe, have been wintering in Key Biscayne, Fla. where they prepare bakes. The highlight of Foster's career was a special party prepared for then–First Lady, Mrs. Lyndon Johnson.

At left, a hungry crowd watches as canvas tarp is taken off, signaling that the food is ready. Above, nestled on a bed of seaweed is the menu prior to cooking: Hotdogs, clams, corn, lobsters, Bermuda onions, potatoes. String attached to test potato, lets cook pull it out to check on cooking progress.

Notes for a Small Clambake

If you want to serve up to eight people, you can use a large enamel pot, and cook over a stove or barbecue grill at home, or take the pot to a picnic area where grills are available. (You can also buy a clam steamer at hardware stores in areas where clambakes are popular. These large pots come in 16 or 20 quart sizes, have two separate compartments for the food, and a spigot at the bottom for draining off the clam juice and water.) If you use a large pot, line its bottom with a couple of inches of seaweed and add a quart of water. Place a test potato close to the edge of the pot where it won't disturb the other food ingredients when you pull it out. Add the rest of the food in the same order you would for a large bake and pack seaweed around the top and sides of the inside of the pot. Then cover and cook until the test potato tells you the food is done. Combine the broth of water and clam juice with melted butter to make a dip or spread for the food.

There are no rigid rules for having a clambake. Small groups of 6 to 8 people can enjoy a feast of clams, corn, potatoes, onions and lobsters, steamed in large kettles as explained in the text at left. Groups of several dozen or more will need a larger cooking setup, similar to the above-ground "pit" shown on page 468. This is particularly true if the group wants a more elaborate meal, including chicken, hotdogs and, perhaps, some local food specialty such as conch.

A good cooking site for the above-ground pit would be a graveled backyard space, an empty lot or a beach area, if the owner's permission can be obtained by your club or community group. To build the pit, you will need 16 cement cinder blocks (or an equivalent volume of rocks), and a 4 by 8 foot sheet of steel (or a discarded car hood with its paint and grease burned off). For holding the food while it cooks, build a bin consisting of a 2½ by 3½ by 1 foot scrap wood frame with a hardware cloth bottom. A 4 by 5 foot canvas tarp, a smaller section of tarp to tuck around the food in the bin, enough rope to tie the large tarp down over the food bin, a bucket for water used to dampen the seaweed and tarp, a kettle for melting butter, containers for carrying food, an apron, work gloves (to protect against heat and lobsters), and a pitchfork complete the list of cooking accessories needed for clambaking. In addition, for each bake, you will need: about ¼ cord of dry wood and some newspapers to help start the wood burning; and about 3 bushels of wetted-down seaweed. (Corn husks, long grass, Irish moss, palmetto leaves or other plants can be used instead.) You will also need small cheesecloth bags (available from hardware stores) to hold your clams and the two test potatoes you will use to show you when the food is ready.

Calculating Food Portions

Then, of course, there is the all-important food. For each adult guest at a typical clambake, plan on serving: 1 pint of clams; 1 lobster and/or ½ chicken; 1 or 2 ears of corn; 1 or 2 potatoes; 1 or 2 hotdogs; a couple of small onions; and ½ cup of butter or margarine. If you think the guests will have room for dessert (and they usually do) add watermelons to your shopping list. And don't forget the liquid refreshments; seafood and open-air cooking can raise quite a thirst. To serve the food, you will need sturdy, non-absorbent paper plates, large heat-resistant paper cups for the clams and small ones for the melted butter, plenty of napkins, and hand-sized rocks for each guest to use for cracking the lobsters open.

To set up the pit, line up the cinder blocks in two parallel rows about

1: The walls of the bake "pit" can be made with cinder blocks (above) or large stones can be used if they are available. Walls should stand 1½ to 2 feet high.

▶ 2: Wood is stacked loosely between the pit walls. Birch burns best, but if not handy, almost any wood will do. If you use a fast-burning wood, remember to keep plenty of it handy.

3: Sixteen-year-old Mark Foster gathers Maine rockweed (a form of seaweed) shortly
before the bake. But you need not live in Maine to enjoy your steamers.
In other parts of the country, use other greenery.

4: First layer on top of sheet-metal is
rockweed, spread 6 to 8 inches deep. Whatever greenery you find to use, make sure
it is thoroughly wet down for clambake.

5: The four-sided wood and hardware cloth
bin is placed on the seaweed. If you are
serving only a small number of people—
say, six—bin isn't necessary.

4 feet apart, photograph 1. If you use rocks instead of blocks, make sure they
are stacked to a height of 1½ to 2 feet. Between these walls, loosely pile
your firewood to a height of about 1 foot, as shown in photograph 2; this
will leave space for the fire to breathe. Lay the steel sheet on top of the
two block walls, as in photograph 4. Spread a 6- to 8-inch deep layer of wet
seaweed on top of the metal sheet. Then center the food bin on top of the
seaweed, photograph 5. Place two test potatoes, each in a separate cheesecloth bag, at diagonally opposite corners on the wire bottom of the bin. Make
sure the strings attached to each bag are long enough to trail down over the
sheet metal's edge, so that you can reach them comfortably.

Since the bottom of the bin will be hottest, the foods that normally take
the longest to cook make up the first or bottom layer you put in the bin. For

7: Properly placed in the bin, the food is ready for baking. Note clams in cheesecloth bags, and string in lower left corner leading from test potato.

8: Because of abundance of ingredients stacked in the bin to feed more than a dozen people, Foster uses small canvas tarp to keep food from scattering.

9: Another 2 to 3 inches more seaweed on top of the small tarp helps retain the heat and moisture. Now the fire can be started, and steam will begin to generate.

6: Mark Foster adds corn ears, still in their husks, to the trough. Ingredients requiring the longest baking times go in first; those that cook quickly, last.

this particular bake, that means that the potatoes and Bermuda onions go in first. Next comes the chicken (cut in half and thoroughly defrosted if purchased whole or frozen). Next are the lobsters, and then the corn (still in its husks), together with the hotdogs. The clams, dropped into cheesecloth bags to keep them from being scattered among the other foods, make up the final layer in the bin. If you are baking for a large group and your food bin is tightly packed, it may help to tuck the food snugly into its bin with a small tarp. This will help hold the food in its bin and keep it separated from the seaweed. It will also help contain heat and moisture. But the small tarp is optional. Whether or not you use the extra tarp, you should cover the food (or small tarp) with a layer of seaweed, about 2 to 3 inches deep. Then top this final layer of seaweed with a tarp large enough to be tied down around the food bin to help retain the moisture and heat.

Light Your Fire
With the food bin filled and the large, outer tarp tied over it, you can light your fire and let the cooking begin. Make sure your bucket of water is handy; the fire will dry out your weeds and tarp so they need re-wetting in order to keep the steam generating. And it is the steam that does the cooking. The clams will open after some 20 minutes of steaming. That's when they start letting their savory juices seep down over the foods below them, giving the meal its distinctive clambake flavor.

Hungry though you may be, you must wait from 40 to 60 minutes after your fire is well under way for the food to be ready. The precise time will depend on how hot the fire is and how much food you are cooking. That's why you have the two test potatoes. After 40 or 50 minutes, pull out one of the test potatoes; if it crushes easily, your bake is done. If it is still hard, wait until 50, 60 or even 70 minutes have passed (depending on how hard the first potato was), and then try the second test potato. It should be done; if not, allow a little more cooking time before you serve the food. It is important that you keep the fire up and the steam generating from the seaweed throughout the cooking process.

10: A second, larger canvas tarp, wetted down, is tossed over the trough and weeds. Anchored with rope to pit base, it keeps steam from dissipating too quickly, thus conserving firewood.

11: The fire kept burning briskly and seaweed occasionally wet down as it dries, this clambake should be ready to eat in about an hour. For this particular bake, pit walls built up of locally available stones were used.

Serving the Bake

Just a few minutes before you expect the food to be done, put your butter or margarine in a kettle and set the kettle on the edge of the metal sheet, as in photograph 12. The melted butter will be used with the clams, lobsters, potatoes and corn. Then, as soon as a test potato indicates all is ready, serve the food as quickly as possible. Food—particularly clams—served in

12: Begin melting butter at sheet-metal edge a few minutes before you expect bake to be done. Melted butter can be poured from kettle into paper cups.

13: Pull test potato from bin after 40 or 50 minutes. If it crumbles easily, bake is ready. If not, cook another 10 or 20 minutes and try the second test potato.

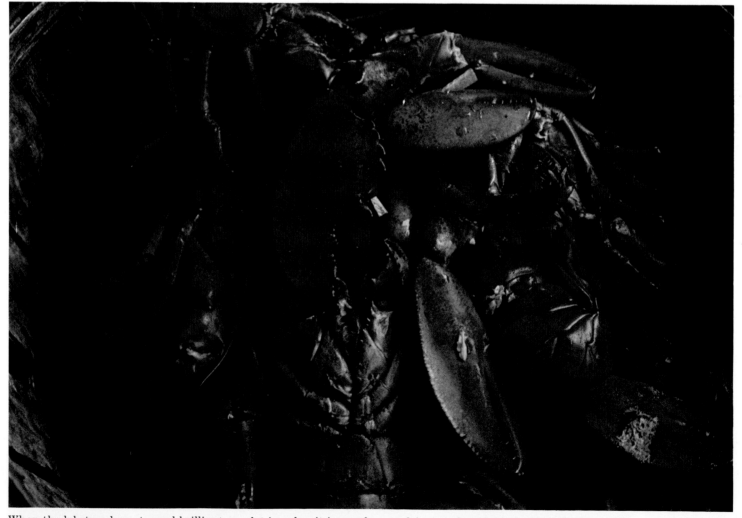

When the lobsters have turned brilliant scarlet in color, it is another useful sign that the bake is ready for eating.

the open air cools rapidly. The assembly-line method of serving works well, with all the corn in one pan or basket, all the potatoes in another, all the onions in another, and so forth. The clams can be served directly out of their cheesecloth bags.

Self-Service Lineup Best

Have the guests line up with paper plates in hand and help themselves to the corn, potatoes, chicken, onions, lobsters and hotdogs. The clams can be served in large, heat-resistant paper cups and the melted butter in smaller ones. Pour the butter directly from the kettle you heated it in, to save a mess. Make sure everyone has hand-sized rocks; these will be used for cracking open the lobster shells. This method works amazingly well and is lots of fun, particularly for the younger guests. (But just to be on the safe side—if you think some of the guests will be fussy about how they eat their lobsters or will have difficulty with the rock crushing—it might be wise to have a few nutcrackers, pliers and lobster forks available for those who ask for them.)

Dessert should be simple and portable. As mentioned earlier, watermelon is a good choice, and it should be served just when the clambakers are recovering from their first course. The choice of beverages is up to you—whatever you think the majority of the group will prefer. If you plan to serve coffee after the feast, it can be made in advance and heated up on the metal sheet while the first course is underway.

This youngster agrees that watermelon makes an ideal dessert for a clambake. But other fruits may also be used.

14: Wear work gloves and take care in lifting steaming food from bin. Sort food by type in separate containers, from which guests can serve themselves.

15: A pitchfork will enable you to clear your steel sheet of hot weed which should be spread on the ground to cool. Weed can later be used as a fertilizer.

Cleaning Up

Once you've taken the baked food from the bin, lift the bin from its steaming weed bed. Be careful not to touch the hot metal hardware cloth or steel sheet. Use a pitchfork to lift the weed off the steel sheet. Spread the weed about on the ground so that it can cool quickly. Then reach under the sheet metal with the pitchfork, directly into the pit, and spread the wood and ashes as much as you can. By the time you've finished eating, the material you used to build your pit will be cool enough to handle.

Try to leave your bake area as clean and natural as you found it. This is especially important if you baked on a beach or lake shore. If you moved rocks to construct your pit base, scatter them again. With your pitchfork, scrape as much of the wood ash as you can into the sand or ground, and bury the charcoal. The weed you used can be saved for fertilizer or taken to the nearest dump or trash can along with the garbage that has accumulated. Obviously, your food bin, sheet-metal, tarps, and cement cinder blocks should be saved for your next big clambake.

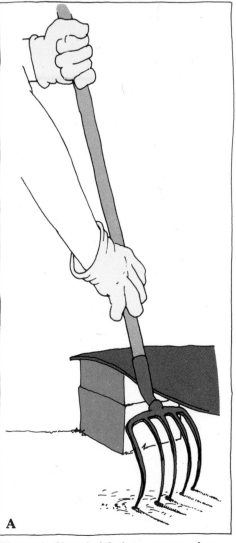

Figure A: Use pitchfork to scrape ashes into ground around the clambake site.

16: The clam's air hole is easily identified. Start to dig on one side of the hole and work your way toward it.

17: Crumble—don't rake—the wet sand with short, choppy strokes a few inches deep. Work your way past the hole.

18: As the rake churns up the sand, look for the clam, which can be anywhere within a few inches of its hole.

19: Place clam in a slat-bottomed trough. Continue to chop sand along the beach where siphon holes appear.

This fully-equipped clam digger walks toward a Maine beach with his tools in hand. Regulations for clamming vary in different localities but permits are required.

Clamming

Although you can order clams from your local fish or specialty food store, you might consider a clamming expedition to get you into a clambake mood. The edible clam most popular with those living along the Atlantic Coast is the soft-shell. It is also called the steamer or long-neck (because of its long siphon). Soft-shell clams are usually 2 to 4 inches in diameter, and have thick but brittle shells that are often chalky white but may be stained by the ground. The harder-shelled quahog or littleneck clams, found from southern Canada to Florida, are 4 to 5 inches in diameter when grown. They are grayish outside and whitish inside, usually with one deep purple edge. When small, they are known as cherrystone clams. Quahogs can be kept refrigerated for several weeks but soft-shell clams should be eaten promptly.

An edible clam found on both coasts is the razor clam, about 6 or 7 inches long and 1 inch across. Other West Coast favorites include the pismo and the large geoduck, which is considered a real delicacy.

The tools you will need for clamming are a clam rake and a slat-bottomed trough. Both are available at hardware stores near clamming areas. You will also need a permit for clamming, usually available at the local town hall. When you pick up the permit, ask where the best clam beds are, and whether any areas have been posted off-limits because of water pollution. Clams can be collected more easily when the tide is low. So also ask to see a tide table you can check for the best clamming times.

When you reach your clamming beach, look around for the telltale holes made by the clams' siphons. Each hole will be a deep indentation, about ½ inch in diameter, that stands out against the smooth beach. Dig the rake's teeth into the mud a few inches on your side of the hole and drag it toward you, crumbling the sand as you go. Work toward the hole, keeping a sharp eye out for the clam. When you find it, make sure it is regulation size, and, if it is, put it into your slat-bottomed trough. When you've dug your limit of clams, wash them by jiggling the trough around in the water. Then take them home to eat and remember that they're tastiest if cooked the same day.

For related projects and techniques see the entries, "American Indian Crafts," "Beachcombing," "Canoeing," "Sails and Sailing," "Shells."

▶ 20: When you've filled the trough, wash the sand clinging to the clams by dipping the container in the sea and gently agitating it. The rake and trough are the only tools needed and can be found in any hardware store in the clamming area. A bucket with holes punched through the bottom might be substituted for the clam trough.

▼ Clamming is done in the area of beach exposed by low tide, anywhere below the high water mark. It's backbreaking work and often takes hours, but the rewards are great. It's also messy, so wear old clothes and prepare to get very dirty. Before you start, be sure to check local regulations about permits and minimum clam size.

COLLAGES AND ASSEMBLAGES
Art from Scraps

Barbara Auran-Wrenn is a designer who writes for many magazines. Her designs are influenced by her interest in folk art. She experiments with many materials, including found objects, which she uses to construct collages and assemblages.

If you have ever made a valentine by pasting up bits of lace and colored paper, you have made a collage. The technique is centuries old and can be traced back to the folk art of making paper cutouts. Until the turn of this century, it was charmingly naive and unselfconscious. In Victorian times, elaborate pictures of bouquets and landscapes were constructed of bristly horsehair. Scrapbooks of the period also were a form of collage, as were handmade children's books stitched with soft, muslin pages, then with pasted pictures from catalogs and magazines. People saved ornate cigar bands and glued them in fancy borders on boxes. Perhaps the most curious examples of collage were the memory jugs whose surfaces were covered with rows of objects, buttons, beads, and packed communities of tiny dolls. Another example is encountered in folk paintings on which actual objects, such as seashells and butterflies, were pasted to represent themselves. Perhaps the artist used this device hoping to fool the eye, or to hide lack of skill.

This collage includes waves cut from colored tissue paper, illustrations from children's picture books, old postcards, an old blueprint, decorated cardboard poker chips, a section of folding ruler, and a cloth watchband. All are glued to a wooden board that, with a valance at the top, came from a lumberyard scrap pile. To see an example of a free-standing sculptural assemblage, turn to page 486.

From Painting to Collage

Modern collage began around 1910 when Picasso pasted a piece of newspaper on a drawing. The impact of this creation was enormous and indicated that flat, formal painting was no longer adequate for any creative need. Beginning in 1919, a German artist Kurt Schwitters developed collage into a medium as important as painting. From trash heaps, dust bins and sidewalks, he gathered the castoff materials that went into his little pictures and transformed his ragged scraps into an orderly world. Because of Schwitters and others like him, including observant photographers, we have become aware of the natural collages of papers stuck to the pavement by the rain; parts and pieces of things discarded and useless. Modern derivatives of this art form are pure-paper collages like those of Carol Wald at right, and on pages 480 and 481.

From Collages to Assemblages

Within a few years, Picasso's experiment with paper pasted on a drawing had been expanded to include the addition of real objects. When a collage is made with three-dimensional objects, it is called an assemblage or a construction. With the invention of assemblages, virtually all limitations on creative materials disappeared. Even the concept of working within a picture frame ceased to be important. Today, the words collage and assemblage are becoming almost synonymous, since it is difficult to say where one ends and the other begins. The more purely structural forms, like those by John Myracle on pages 486 and 487, are called assemblages, but many collages now contain some three-dimensional objects.

Collages and assemblages, hovering as they do between painting and sculpture, art and craft, offer the unskilled craftsman a point of entry into the fine arts. Since the objects are merely collected and fastened to a surface, usually by gluing, pegging, or nailing, no special training is required in the techniques of drawing perspectives, curves, rounds, and the other phenomena of representational and nonrepresentational painting. In fact, much that an artist working with paint attempts to reproduce on a flat surface is inherent in the dimension, color, and form of an object fastened to a surface.

Materials and Inspiration

Since the techniques used in making collages and assemblages are simple—gluing, pegging, and nailing—the art lies in the selection and arrangement of materials, and it must be personal. You won't want to reproduce exactly some other artist's painting. Training and experience teach one an awareness of the potential of objects. For Schwitters, the sidewalk and trash heap furnished useful materials. The collages and assemblages on the next pages indicate some of the sources of inspiration for contemporary artists.

For the artist, a collage usually begins with a series of questions. Standing in a lumberyard, looking at a magazine or old greeting cards, the artist broods: Will bits of wood, fixed to a board, make a statement, evoke a mood? Will one picture, added to another, become something else? What will happen if different textures and shapes are treated this way? Bit by bit, an idea for a finished work begins to simmer. It is something like the thoughts that go through your mind when you doodle.

In looking at the discards around us for ways in which to change and combine or recombine them, many qualities attract us. We consider the object's design and color; we notice its textures—surfaces are smooth or rough, bright or dull. Some things appear fragile and delicate, others massive and heavy. Much of the excitement of making collages comes from being able to combine these different qualities in a variety of ways to tell a story, state a theme, evoke a mood, startle or please with imaginative new symbiotic or suggestive effects. Collages are truly an art form that is unfettered by conventional materials and formal techniques. What we often discover in making collages and assemblages is our personal reaction to things around us. In creating, we discover ourselves.

A Christmas card in the collage technique called "pure-paper" has no three-dimensional elements at all. It is made of cut-outs gathered from magazines and from old greeting cards. Its creator, artist Carol Wald, whose work appears on pages 480 and 481, has used a combination of the two methods—glue-under and glue-over, illustrated on those pages—to produce this work.

Designs and Decorations
Pure-paper collage

Pure-paper collage teaches the beginner a lot about the composition techniques involved in collages and assemblages and is a good way to get started.

Material and Tools: to cut, sharp-edge artist's knife and blades, straightedge ruler; to cut on, heavy chipboard, 22 by 30 inches; to outline positions of pictures, No. 2 soft lead pencil; to glue, rubber cement; to mount finished collages, pad of 11-by-14-inch Bristol-board sheets; to file a collection of potential collage pictures, 11-by-14-inch folders.

Your picture collection should include lots of large color pictures from magazines, greeting cards, postcard reproductions. File according to type: people, places, objects, backgrounds, and so on. To make a good collage, you need as wide a selection of pictures as possible and a willingness to use them to create dreamlike compositions.

The two major techniques used in collages are illustrated in the color pictures on these pages: the glue-over technique and the glue-under technique.

Carol Ward, a painter and portrait artist as well as a collage artist, exhibits at the Dintenfass Gallery and has a studio in the So-Ho section New York City. Her work is represented in five major museums, and collages have appeared in many publications, such as Time *and* Life, Saturday Review, *and the* New York Times.

1: Use a sharp-pointed artist's knife to cut cleanly when preparing pictures for collages. Change the blade as soon as it dulls. Cutting is done on chipboard.

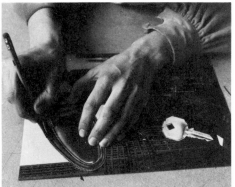

2: With sharp No. 2 lead pencil, outline on the base picture the position of cut-out pictures selected to be glued under or over the base picture.

Glue-over technique of collage begins with the selection of a large picture. This will be the base on which a fanciful assortment of cut-out objects is placed, as here.

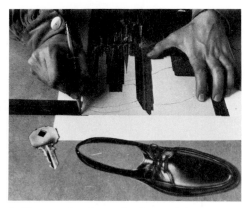

3: Use a ruler to center base picture squarely on Bristol board; pencil-mark corners. Glue this picture to the board before gluing on secondary pictures.

4: To glue pictures, completely cover with a light coat of rubber cement all surfaces (including edges) to be joined. Let dry one minute before gluing down.

Glue-under technique of collage creates a picture in which you view one image through another. Here, the flower picture is glued under cut-out portions of the head.

To make a glue-over collage, begin by selecting about 15 appealing pictures of objects. The choice should be as random as possible. Cut out carefully, as in photograph 1. Select a full-page picture, and place the cutouts on it anywhere you like. Experiment with placement, and have fun with your ideas. Following the instructions for photographs 2 to 4, outline the placement of the objects on the base picture; then mount the base picture on Bristol board, and glue on objects selected.

A glue-under collage is made in the same way. Select the top picture first; cut away the unwanted portions; then slide other pictures under the cut-out portions until you have a composition that appeals to you. Then mount the secondary picture on Bristol board, and glue on the top picture. The result is a picture in which you view one image through another.

Designs and Decorations
Scrap lumber collage

$ ⏱ 👫 🔬

The assemblage shown opposite is a playful composition of wood scraps, with some movable parts that let you redesign it at will. I used a ½-by-36-by-36-inch piece of plywood as the "canvas" for the composition, a 36-inch length of ½-inch dowel to peg the movable pieces to the plywood, wood drapery rings, wood spools and balls, fabric dyes, rubber gloves, tongs, newspapers, an 8-ounce bottle of white glue, a pint of white enamel, a 2-inch brush, saber saw, drill with ½-inch bit, medium sandpaper, and a large cooking pot.

To make the plywood mounting board more interesting, a free-form design was traced on one side and sawed out with a saber saw, as in photograph 1. Then the rough edges were sanded, and it was painted with white enamel. Next, I sanded a random selection of wood scraps in varying sizes and shapes, as in photograph 6, and dyed them different colors, photograph 7.

With the plywood laid flat, I tried various shapes and combinations of wood scraps, drapery rings, pegs, and wood balls, (photograph 8) until I found a basic, balanced composition. The next decision was which pieces should be glued to the board to form a basic design, which should be movable, and which should be glued together, photograph 9. Then ½-inch holes for pegs were drilled into the board and halfway into, or all the way through

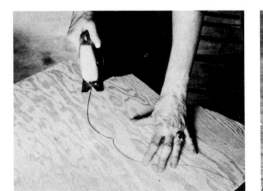

5: A saber saw is used to cut out a decorative free-form curve. This will relieve mounting board's squared-off look.

6: All wood scraps are sanded to remove roughness, then sorted into groups according to the colors they will be dyed.

7: An envelope of dye is stirred into 4 or 5 quarts of boiling water. With tongs each scrap is dunked for a minute.

8: With the mounting board flat, mixtures of shapes and colors are tried until a pleasing arrangement appears. Then it is decided which parts will be fixed, which movable.

the backs of the movable pieces. From the dowel, I cut pegs, varying the lengths to fit the number of wood scraps that would hang on each peg. The pegs were dyed in colors that seemed right for their places in the composition. Then the basic design pieces were glued to the board and the pegs into their holes in the plywood. With the movable pieces in a pleasing arrangement on the pegs, the assemblage will be complete.

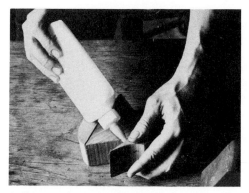

9: Scraps that are glued together should have enough contact area to make a strong joint and not be too heavy for the peg.

10: A drill with ½-inch bit makes peg holes. Hold wood firmly by hand or clamped in a vise. Most holes are drilled halfway through.

With the basic elements glued in place, and pegs for movable parts fixed to the "canvas" the composition awaits the artist's final decisions. The pieces at the foot of the "canvas" belong on the pegs: where would you put them?

William Accorsi intended to become a football coach, but other interests led him into sculpture, collage, designing one-of-a-kind furniture, and writing puzzles. His work is seen in major U.S. galleries. He lives in New York City where he has his own shop.

Designs and Decorations
Cigar box assemblage

$ ⏱ 🚶 🧨

The assemblage at right is probably the busiest cigar box you have ever seen. The box is mounted on the wall with its lid hanging down, and it overflows with activity. A china doll presides as a kind of master of ceremonies, with one arm outstretched toward the time (half past eight) and the other toward the keys. Many faces look out at you, yet who could decipher what is behind their expressions? Indeed, like an unlocked trunk, the box shows you its contents, but you are left to guess at its boundless secrets.

The idea of using a cigar box as a background is excellent, because a box provides a ready-made framework within which to work. The arrangement of matchboxes and pictures supports the illusion of many compartments. At the same time, compartmental boundaries are exploded by the wild mixture of shapes, colors, and the cluster of pieces from a child's game arrayed unevenly around the top.

You can adapt your own found objects to such a cigar-box assemblage. Construction is primarily a matter of gluing to the box and its lid, after you have worked out the design. In developing the basic composition, start with the largest pieces. Experiment with several arrangements until you have the effect you want. Then glue the larger pieces and start fitting

11: Trim ice-cream sticks with tile cutters or a utility knife to make frames for small pictures or create divisions.

12: Pictures should be glued in place first and frame parts added last, after the final composition has been determined.

13: Putting an assemblage together, Bill Accorsi begins with the larger pieces, which he lays out on the basic composition. Small details are added last.

A sophisticated assemblage, constructed in a wooden cigar box, emanates an atmosphere of memories and treasures, enhanced by the inclusion of childhood objects.

14: A good composition is the key to a successful assemblage. Before gluing, try several variations of your arrangement.

the smaller pieces in place. If you want to add frames to small pictures, glue the picture to the box or its lid first with white glue, then cut the parts for the frames from ice-cream sticks, and glue them into place.

Other possibilities include mounting several odd-shaped small boxes on a board and filling the boxes with objects. Sturdy cardboard gift boxes can be sprayed with enamel paint and used this way. For an assemblage with many small compartments, consider painted muffin tins mounted in clusters. A small item such as a marble, shell or stone may be glued in each cup, making every object individually important. String, dipped in liquid starch and dried, provides sturdy partitions when glued on a backing to outline areas. Emphasize by pasting in brilliant papers or fabrics.

John Myracle is a self-taught sculptor who works largely in the medium of assemblage. His work has been exhibited widely, and he has received numerous awards. He is a member of the Connecticut Academy of Fine Arts and lives in Somers, Conn.

Designs and Decorations
Free-form assemblages $$ 🕐 🚶 ⚗

The assemblages here illustrate something of the effects and relationships of objects within a sculptural composition. The two on this page were developed after contemplation of old printer's type made of wood and the dismantled parts of an ancient clock. As in the preceding projects, the pieces and parts were mounted on the chosen form or within the chosen frame, and put together by pegging, gluing, or nailing.

Printer's Type Assemblages
The freestanding assemblage at left below almost makes you believe the alphabet continues into the core of the construction, and evokes the atmosphere of old-time print shops. Massiveness, grayed colors, and something of the labor of putting hand type together are communicated to us through the weight and precision of the letters on their blocks of wood. Big letters juxtaposed with smaller ones make the composition dynamic and portentous, giving balance and pace to the design.

In the assemblage below, weathered wood and clock parts, added to old

15: Free-form assemblage of old printer's type is supported on a piece of 2-by-4 cut at an angle so one side is 5 inches long, the other 3, and joined to the base, a 4¾-by-3¼-inch letter ""U"", by a length of ⅜-inch dowel, fitted and glued into a drilled socket. The other letters were glued to the 2-by-4 with epoxy cement.

Framed assemblage adds clock parts and weathered wood to old printer's display type to conjure up an atmosphere that communicates an awareness of the passage of time. The black frame for the composition is ¼-inch-by-2½-inch lathing and the background is weathered barn siding. The overall size is 16 by 34 inches.

Dagwood sandwich is made of urethane kitchen sponges of varying thickness and coarseness. Bread, with edges browned with watercolor, is filled with any food the imagination can turn a sponge into: Onion rings, for instance, are painted rolled sponges, sliced crosswise; the egg slices were made in similar fashion. Sponges were rolled after painting, pinned in place with toothpicks until dry, then sliced.

Craftsman's apprentice at work, circa 1791.

printers' type, suggest the relentless tick of time, the ever-present deadlines faced by printers and editors. You can almost hear the clacking of the presses. To make the structure balance, the clock face is off-center to the left; numbers are staggered to the right in a graceful curve, springs and wheels are set at random as counterpoint to the other elements. Overlap is created by attaching parts with nails of differing lengths.

Exercise in Sponges

The sandwich above is a structural assemblage in a lighter mood. Ever wonder what you could make with a couple of dozen round and rectangular kitchen sponges? This Dagwood special was made from whole or sliced urethane sponges, of varying sizes and coarseness to resemble the size and forms of common sandwich food. Only the lettuce is not a sponge; it is made of crinkled green plastic packing paper. Watercolors, white glue, and toothpicks (to hold wet sponges in place as they dried in shape) were the only other materials used to make the sandwich.

This type of art may not be your favorite, but it is fun, and it frees the imagination to seek new forms and ideas in commonplace household objects.

For related projects, see the entries "'Boxes," "Cardboard," Decoupage," "Papercrafts," "Preschool Projects," and "Valentines."

COLONIAL CRAFTS
Life in Early America

Melissa Schnirring gained her inspiration for this article about life in the early days of rural New England during a lengthy stay at the restoration in Sturbridge, Mass. In Old Sturbridge Village, Colonial life is faithfully recreated in its seasonal rounds by employees hired to carry out the tasks Colonists once pursued. Melissa and her husband, Bill, have a deep interest in the self-reliant life of the rural Colonists and the crafts they ingeniously learned.

Many crafts that we take up today for recreation or as gainful hobbies filled basic needs for the villager-farmer of rural New England in the late eighteenth and early nineteenth century. A combination of factors left only do-it-yourself or do-without-it alternatives: the isolation often imposed by primitive roads and rough winters, the subsistence (rather than cash crop) farming in remote areas, and the shortage of cash to buy ready-made articles when they were available. It is not easy for today's do-it-yourselfer to grasp the gravity of these alternatives. Truly, sound crafts knowledge made the difference between comfort and bare existence: if you wanted your hands warm during the icy winters, you had to master all the crafts involved in transforming dirty, tangled fleece on a sheep into finished mittens—shearing, carding, spinning, dyeing and knitting.

The New England farmer and his family responded resourcefully to the challenge when the United States was young. They became skilled at handcrafting the articles they needed, using the materials nature provided. Their land was forested, and the trees provided fuel for heating and cooking as well as lumber for buildings, wagons, furniture, barrels, spinning wheels and many other farm and household implements. Trees enriched the family diet by yielding nuts, fruits (for cider and pickling, too) and maple sap for syrup and sugar. The charming little walnut- and apple-face dolls we treasure today were a gift of the forests, too.

In those days the land provided crops that fed the people and their livestock. The livestock in turn gave not only meat, milk, butter and cheese, but wool for clothing, hides for breeches, aprons, caps, boots, buckets, saddles and even drinking mugs, bones for implements, and tallow and grease for candles and soap. The land also furnished herbs for seasoning, flax for clothing, clay for pottery, flowers, leaves, roots, minerals, insects, used for dyeing yarns.

The early New Englander's awareness of nature's bounty and his skill in utilizing it effectively are attributes that we children of technology might well envy today. On the following pages is described a way of life in which crafts played a vital role, filling man's need for both comfort and creativity. That is, essentially, what *The Family Creative Workshop* is all about. Many of these early crafts—candlemaking, spinning, maple syrup and sugarmaking, caning, rush weaving, cheesemaking, patchwork, pipe carving and others—are among the *Workshop*'s entries. Details about sheep shearing and yarn dyeing are explained on pages 496 and 497.

Clothing: Re-enacting life early in the nineteenth century, this Old Sturbridge Village couple (employees of this restoration village) is dressed in Sunday best, ready to attend church or town meeting. Most such clothing was homemade from raw materials prepared by the family. Some items, such as the gentleman's hat, could only be bought in city shops, and were lifelong treasured possessions.

Maple Sugaring: As it was practiced by New England Colonial farmers, maple sugaring is part of the seasonal round in Old Sturbridge Village, Sturbridge, Mass., a museum town that recreates village life in the early days of America. Snow was still on the ground when this first crop of the year, maple sap, was harvested during the early thaws. Note the hollowed logs used to catch the drip, an Indian trick the Colonists learned in the days when buckets were a luxury.

Spinning: This Old Sturbridge Village lady shows how to spin linen yarn from the long inner fibers of the flax plant, gathered on the spindle at the right. The goal is a smooth, even yarn, twisted for strength. Skill is acquired only after much practice.

For a time fix, we have chosen the period between 1790 and 1840. To evoke scenes from rural America of those years, we photographed in Old Sturbridge Village, Sturbridge, Mass. The Village, open to the public, recreates village and farm life of this period. Its inhabitants are paid employees, trained in the early farming and craft techniques.

A Look into the Past

As the first half century of the Republic unfolded, the inland rural New England family was an industrious, nearly self-sufficient unit. Of its three main preoccupations (food, clothing and housing), only clothing was not governed by the seasons. Clothmaking was a year-round craft.

Farm life was hard on clothes, almost all of which had to be made at home. A ripped garment meant for a woman one more mending chore that night by the light of the fire or by a burning pine or hemlock knot or tow-wick candle. Nothing that could be repaired was ever discarded. What was worn out became part of something else—an appliqued quilt or a braided rug, for instance, or a patchwork pillow. The constant need for production didn't keep the women from adding touches of grace to their needlework. While not a scrap of cloth could be wasted, simple patchwork, pieces and appliqued, gradually evolved into a folk art of extraordinary originality and beauty.

Babies came along to add to the family's need for cloth, but as they grew, they added hands to fashion it, too. Girls learned to knit with homespun yarns when they were about four years old, to spin homegrown flax into linen thread when they were six. Men, women, and children wove cloth on looms. Boys even took small looms along when they pastured the sheep, weaving while they watched over the herd. From the wool and linen cloth, the women sewed clothes and produced the quilts, rugs, towels, curtains, napkins, and other articles for the home.

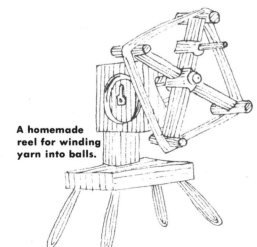

A homemade reel for winding yarn into balls.

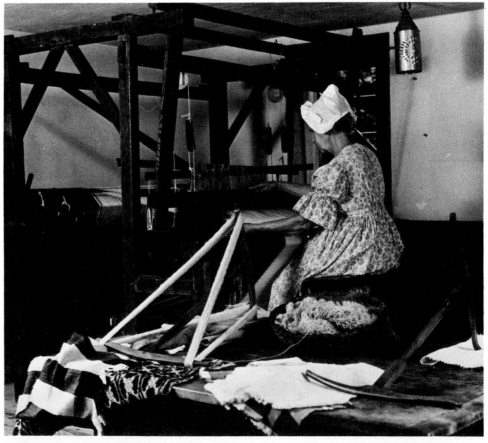

Weaving: A year-round task that fell to Colonial women was weaving from farm-grown flax clothing and such items as napkins and table scarfs shown in foreground.

Plowing: Today's Old Sturbridge Village farmers show how to plow with oxen, as did our ancestors. Oxen could keep their footing on New England's rocky, rough slopes and in half-drained swales. They were also used for hauling, stump pulling, other heavy work.

The family managed to combine sociability with cloth production. Women took their spinning wheels when they visited neighbors and they organized the quilting and spinning bees that whiled away the hours that could be spared from the year's round of farming activities.

Spring

For the majority of the family's activities, the seasons called the tune in early rural New England. Late winter or early spring when the sap rose, was the time for making maple syrup and sugar—although a capricious January thaw could send a farmer out through deep snowdrifts to tap his maples. The Indians, whose generosity in helping the early settlers is rarely acknowledged, had taught the farmers to cut V-shape slashes low on the tree trunks and insert a piece of birch bark in each slash to funnel the sap. The farmers improved on this, if a hand auger was available, by drilling into the trunk and replacing the birch bark with a hollow tube.

Spring was also the time for sheep shearing and much of the planting. New England farms were 50 to 200 acres in size at this time, but only half a dozen of these acres on each would be in crops at one time, with perhaps twice that much in meadows or in partly cleared permanent pasture for swine and cattle. With the primitive implements available around 1800, it was a very hard day's work to plow an acre and even slower, backbreaking labor to harvest it. A farmer thought twice before he planted additional acreage, especially if he didn't have a ready market for the surplus—that is, if he didn't live near a sizable town or at least close to a river, by far the best means of transportation in those days.

Maize (Indian corn) was the basic crop and the basic foodstuff for farm families and, along with hay, for livestock winter feed. Hard work breeds hearty appetites, but our educated palates today would surely rebel at such an incessant onslaught of corn: corn mush (hasty pudding), boiled corn, roasted corn, corn meal baked into corn cake and corn pudding. (And the husks made cornhusk dolls!) A blight of parasites harbored in barberry bushes had wiped out wheat crops by 1800 in all New England except Vermont and along the western borders. This meant the virtual disappearance of white bread; the substitute was corn meal and rye flour bread called "rye and Injun."

Churning Butter: It required little skill but lots of elbow grease to keep the wooden handle moving up and down until the butter solidified. Churning was one of the many chores that kept housewives busy throughout the year.

A primitive but ingenious eggbeater. The beater shaft turns as the string looped once around it is moved back and forth.

491

Besides corn, the farmer planted hay, together with a shade crop of oats, in the spring. (The hay would not be ready for harvest until the following year, but the oats would be ready in August.) He also planted flax to provide the fibers from which the women spun thread for the weaving of cloth. Potatoes and the kitchen garden (including most of the vegetables we know today except for the tomato) went in as soon as the earth warmed, along with herbs, destined for the meat stews that would provide some variation from the eternal diet of corn. Throughout the growing season, as each crop ripened, there would be preserving and pickling chores for the women and girls, as well as jams to make to stock the larder against winter.

Summer

The frantic pace of the spring planting season eased a little as the weather warmed. Though there were hay, rye, and oats to be harvested and potatoes for everyone to help dig, other chores sent the family ranging the countryside, and these were more like diversions. Fishing was a legitimate chore, and snaring added to the variety summer brought to meals. In the hot, lazy days of midsummer, there were berries to gather, first raspberries and wild strawberries, then blueberries. There were sweet-smelling herbs to seek, for strewing on the church benches and for making little dried nosegays to scent drawers and linen stores. Other herbs were for medicinal uses, and other berries, nuts, and barks (maple, walnut, and oak) for the dyeing of yarns.

For the farmer, as the kitchen garden grew, there was the special joy of watching over, nurturing, harvesting, and drying the seeds of those vegetables that were the best of the year's crop, to provide good seed for the next year's sowing. As the season waxed, then waned, the family began to collect the materials that made the winter months' craft production possible —the right piece of wood to carve a toy, a staircase railing, or a spindle;

Haying: Lacking mechanical aids such as mowers and balers, the early American harvested hay for his livestock by hand, using hand-made implements.

A homemade wooden fork for pitching hay

Candle Dipping: Simple but time-consuming, the making of candles by hand was best done outdoors because it was a messy, smelly chore done over an open fire. The number of dips determined the candles' size and lasting power.

perhaps special boards to bend and smooth for a cradle for the baby to come, rushes for winter basketmaking, a gnarled brier root for a pipe, stalks of broomcorn for a new broom.

Summer was the time for home improvement on a large scale. These were the years when rural New Englanders were beginning to turn their log cabins into buildings for livestock and were constructing frame houses for their families. In more remote areas, they still hewed the beams (oak in New York, maple in Vermont, chestnut elsewhere if it was more plentiful) and sawed the boards by hand (white pine for flooring and siding), but sawmills now began to appear on every New England river. A nailmaking machine had been invented, so nails were no longer rare and expensive. After weeks (with a sawmill nearby) or months of preparation, neighbors were summoned to help join and raise the frame for the new house. This was always a festive occasion, with outdoor tables groaning with food and drink prepared by the new home owners for all the helping hands.

All was not unrelieved toil for the farm family, especially as the nineteenth century progressed. Depending on the severity of the customs of the district, there was fun to be had. Bees were organized for men as well as women—to clear a field of stumps, to raise a house, to augment a farmer's lumber supply, and, most popular of all, to husk maize. After a cornhusking, there was always time for athletic contests. Hunting, fishing, skating and swimming in season were popular with men. There were Training Day with its public shooting matches (later replaced by Independence Day), boisterous Election Day, County Court Day, and the agricultural fairs of the early 1800s.

Fall

With autumn came the last urgent preparations for the months ahead, when the land would lie still under its winter blanket, and warmth and food would depend on the industry and wisdom of the preceding seasons. There was corn to be harvested, rye for the following year to be sown. The last of the fruits and vegetables had to be picked and stored, dried or pickled, or preserved.

The men did the heaviest work, but for the women it was a time of almost frenzied activity. The fall crop of apples had to be sliced and hung on long strings from the rafters to dry, or else stored in barrels in the cellar, straw separating the layers to avoid that one bad apple that could spoil the lot. The last of the garden crops were stored—potatoes, turnips, onions, beets, cabbage, parsnips, carrots, squash, pumpkins, pears, whatever would keep.

Autumn brought butchering time, and for a few weeks there was fresh meat. Most of it had to be pickled in brine, though some of it was smoked or dried, for future use. Animal fat was rendered into tallow for candles, which had to be made outdoors. The women raced against time to prepare a good supply while the fair weather (Indian summer, if they were fortunate) lasted. They slipknotted candlewicks onto candle rods and dipped them, with intervals for cooling, as many as 40 times into the tallow in a large iron cauldron over an open fire. They also used animal fat for soapmaking, combining it with lye from leached ashes. Some dyeing had to be done in the fall, too, yellow from goldenrod or onions, for example.

The men threshed the harvested rye on the barn floor with a flail, separating the grain from the straw, then winnowed it outdoors in a shallow bowl, tossing the grain in the air so the wind could blow away the chaff. Silage corn for the livestock was cut and stored in September. Corn intended for human consumption was tied in bunches or shocks and left in the fields to dry and harden. Later on, some of it was brought in, husked, shelled (in some cases with a flail, but usually with a knife or crank-operated corn sheller), and taken to the nearest mill for grinding into corn meal. Some shocks were left in the fields until needed in winter.

Winter

Once the flying snows of winter had locked in the last pasture, important indoor tasks were waiting: the ever-present cloth production; repairing or

Broommaking: With the aid of this primitive but efficient binding machine, the Colonial broommaker could produce ten or twelve sturdy brooms in an hour.

A Colonial broom made of broomcorn stalks.

Log Splitting: Colonial farmers often split logs for boardmaking by hand, but they took advantage of any available riverside sawmills to cut wood for houses, barns, fences, tools, and furniture.

making tools, implements, and furniture; mending boots and shoes (more likely the former—the virgin forest and mossy topsoil, now eroded, held moisture like a sponge, and the farmer almost always wore boots); repairing harnesses; lacing together cracked or broken pottery with linen thread; and, as spring approached, husking and shelling corn (always the best ears with the straightest rows of kernels were set aside for planting) and threshing grain for the coming sowing.

But the farm family was by no means locked in. Quite the opposite. The snows smoothed the primitive roads and made sleighing parties feasible, trips to town easier (some towns even used rollers to pack down the road snow) and visits to distant friends possible. Families packed and came to stay for days and perhaps for weeks, catching up on all that had happened since the previous year. And even if they stayed at home, there was time during the frozen months for a man to carve that brier pipe, for a woman to cross-stitch a sampler, for a daughter to augment her hope chest.

The snow also opened the way for a chore that rivaled cloth production for

Blacksmithing: Old Sturbridge Village's faithful reproduction of a Colonial blacksmith's shop includes a lever-operated, overhead bellows and the wide variety of tongs and other tools needed for forging and tempering metal.

its absolute necessity: getting in firewood for the year. Farm life required firewood in awesome quantities. The kitchen fireplace or stove was always wood hungry. In a large house, a fireplace or stove in the parlor used wood in winter. Dyeing, soapmaking and the smokehouse consumed a lot of wood in autumn. And in season, maple sugaring created a tremendous demand, since the farmer had to boil down 35 to 40 gallons of the maple sap to get one gallon of maple syrup. With further boiling, he got about eight pounds of maple sugar from one gallon of syrup. In the early 1800s, a hundred-acre farm often produced as much as 1,000 pounds of sugar a year.

Wood was cut in winter because the task was easier then, on both man and beast. The snow cover made hauling lighter because there was less drag on the sled runners. (Sleds were used for year-round hauling, due to the shortage and expense of wheels.) At first, farmers used a broadax for the cutting of wood and, later on, a two-man saw (no doubt reflecting on the wisdom of the saying that wood was the fuel that warmed you twice, once when you cut it and

Tinsmithing: A tinsmith solders together cut tin pieces, then forms them with hand tools, just as the Colonists did. Early tinsmiths not only produced table and storage vessels, but mended them.

once when you burned it). Frozen wood split more easily, too, and wood cut when the sap wasn't running was less prone to insect attack and more secure for building.

Do-It-Yourself to Fix-It-Yourself

The intense round of seasonal activities on which comfort and even survival depended did not ease as the nineteenth century progressed, but the rural New England farmer's means of coping with them did. In 1790, he was quite likely to make his own boots, hammer out spades and two-tined forks on his own anvil and make whatever new furniture was required. The combined efforts of the men and women produced everything they needed except coffee, tea, spices, molasses, salt and sugar; of these, only salt was indispensable. The local store carried these commodities, in addition to fancier forms of dry goods than the women could make from wool and flax. The farmer could pay for his purchases in cash if he had it or exchange surplus he had produced: cheeses, grain, flaxseed, hides, tallow, lumber, pork, beef, wood ashes.

By the turn of the century, however, peddlers began to carry all sorts of wares to the most remote districts. Visits by traveling artisans became frequent enough to take care of many chores, such as hide tanning and bootmaking. As towns grew larger, more specialized shops appeared: a West India goods store, a hardware store, an apothecary shop, and even a millinery shop. Artisans opened shops: blacksmiths, potters, broommakers, pewterers, coopers, cabinetmakers, and tinsmiths, usually part-time farmers themselves.

Basic materials became more plentiful. Iron mines and blast furnaces, up and down the Connecticut River and along the New York-Massachusetts border, were catching up to the demand, and by 1812, there were 160 cotton mills in the tristate area of Connecticut, Rhode Island and Massachusetts.

By 1840, the degree of craft-dependent self-sufficiency required for survival had diminished, but some of the crafts continued to flourish. And some of the products of necessity that the New England farm families crafted (exquisitely appliqued quilts, for example) not only have survived but are on display in museums today.

Pewtermaking: Old Sturbridge Village pewterer heats a spoon mold over a candle. He will pour in the molten pewter, let it cool, strike it loose, smooth and polish it.

Sheep is placed upright, all four legs extended, to keep it still while it is being sheared. Once seated, animal behaves surprisingly well.

Sheep Shearing and Wool Carding

A review of the early steps in the home production of wool yarns shows some of the effort required in Colonial times to provide raw materials for the craftsman. The process of yarnmaking begins with sheep shearing, a painless—to the sheep— but messy job. The process, by the way, has changed little, although today electric shears are used instead of hand shears.

The shearer placed the sheep upright to immobilize it and began shearing at the neck, working down the underside a distance, then cutting up around the neck and head. So he could roll the fleece back as he worked, he pulled the fleece apart along the center of the underside. Working from the underside up around to the back, he sheared from head to tail, rolling the fleece back as he went and being careful not to cut into the roll, which would mean shortened, useless fibers. A similar pulling-apart process was also necessary for each leg, but the result was an entire, intact fleece. It took an hour or more to shear a sheep with the hand clippers used around 1800, and by the end, the shearer's clothing was covered with the lanolin from the sheep's skin.

Preparing the Wool

The oily wool was cleansed in a large kettle in a mixture of one part urine (usually human; urine was one of the few sources of ammonia then) to two parts water. After being rinsed and dried, it was ready for carding.

In Colonial villages, carding was done by hand, at home. The wood had to be picked over to remove bits of dirt, burrs, twigs, and other foreign matter. Then a bit of oil was added to it, and the wool was carefully combed or carded by hand with wooden cards, implements that look like wire brushes. (These can be bought today at craft and hobby shops.) By means of the bristles on the cards, the carder opened the wool fibers then drew them together, combing the wool from one card to the other, forming at last a roll of fluffy strands (see photograph on opposite page.) The wool fibers were then ready for spinning into yarn and dyeing.

Dyeing the Yarn

Before the mid-nineteenth century, basic dyeing was done with such natural substances as dried insects, powdered minerals, roots, flowers, and leaves. When easy-to-use chemical dyes were invented, homemade natural dyestuffs quickly lost popularity. However, a characteristic of natural dyes—the unpredictability of their color—is exactly what makes them appealing to today's home dyers. They produce individual rather than standardized effects on yarn or fabric. No two dye lots are identical.

Some of the natural dye sources that have been used at one period or another can be found in almost every region of the country. Reds and pinks of various shades were obtained from the juices of cherries, strawberries

Old Sturbridge Village shearer demonstrates use of hand shearer, the tool used in Colonial times. Today, shearing is done with electric clippers.

and red raspberries. A reddish purple was made from the berries of common pokeweed. The stalks of sorrel, cardinal flower, red oak and hemlock were also used as sources for reds with a brownish cast. Purple colors were extracted from the juices of wild grapes and wild blueberries. Willow and birch bark were boiled to make rose in a tannish shade, and certain yellows were obtained from willow leaves, marsh marigold, ash bark, tulip tree leaves, ragweed and burdock.

An attractive gold-gray color was obtained by the Colonists from goldenrod. One and a half pecks of goldenrod blossoms, cut near the tops of the stems, were gathered for dyeing one pound of yarn. The blossoms were soaked overnight in water in a large kettle. Next day, they were boiled in water for two hours. After cooling, the mixture was strained through several layers of cheesecloth. On the third day, it was ready to be used for the dye bath.

Other yellow shades were obtained from various other flowers and from dried onion skins. More than half of the natural dyes produced yellows. Browns were obtained from black-walnut hulls and various barks, rusts from madder and other roots, green-grays from many plants, including bayberry, lily-of-the-valley leaves, and sedges. The indigo peddler supplied the blues.

The first step in the dyeing process was mordanting the spun-yarn fibers.

Shorn, the sheep is content to be rid of the hot coat of wool for the summer. The large, intact fleece will be spread out for sorting.

This prepared them to receive the dye, combine with it and form an insoluble compound, thus fixing the color. The Colonists used a mixture of potash alum and cream of tartar or, after 1820, a chrome mordant, all obtainable from village stores. Two huge kettles were suspended over open fires. One held plain water, in which the yarn was presoaked for about an hour; in the other was the warm mordant bath. After soaking, the yarn was transferred to the mordant bath, left for an hour over the fire, then allowed to cool gradually, removed, rinsed in cool water, and hung to dry.

For the dyeing, a large kettle was filled with water and another with four to five gallons of the strained color mixture. As in the mordanting process, the yarn had an hour's presoak in hot water; then it spent an hour in the dye bath, kept just below the boiling point. For rinsing, the yarn went back to the hot-water kettle, and cold water was gradually added until the water was cold. The yarn was then hung to dry.

You can use these same processes today for home dyeing. Search out the

Carding: Two cards, each covered with nail-like teeth, were employed to work pieces of sheared fleece into long rolls of wool fibers. The process eliminated short, unworkable fibers, left the others parallel.

Dyeing: Hanks of yarn spun from carded wool were dyed, then hung to dry. Wool dyeing, like candle dipping, was done outdoors because both generated unpleasant odors.

Wool was placed on one card and brushed lightly with the other until spread evenly. Heavier strokes were then used to return it to the other card, and the process was repeated—and repeated.

natural dye materials in season because the purest colors result from using fresh flower or plant material picked just as it is reaching maturity. Strict adherence to mordanting and dyeing times and temperatures are also required for purity of color. Avoid hard water, which would cause the dye to spot and be irregularly distributed, as would crowding the material in the bath. Finally, the dye kettle itself can affect the colors, "saddening" (dulling) or brightening them: iron kettles tend to dull colors; copper kettles give a brighter color result and brass kettles produce even brighter color. Enameled kettles do not affect color.

Dyeing with natural materials, as the Colonists did produced the subtle, gentle, earthy tones we associate with paintings of the period, and is a fascinating exercise for the modern craftsman. The dyes held well and rarely faded. Although somewhat unpredictable, the colors are appropriate for homespuns and handwoven fabrics. Materials for home dyeing are readily available and easily improvised. More detailed instructions for using the Colonists' natural dyes are included in the entry "Vegetable Dyes."

For related crafts and projects, see the entries "American Indian Crafts," "Beadwork," "Breads," "Cheeses and Churning," "Folk Art," "Herbs," "Pottery," "Quilting," "Sheepskin Coats," "Spinning," and "Weaving."

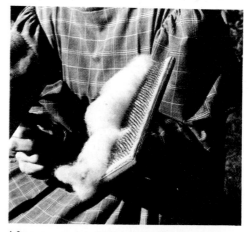

After many repetitions, the wool was at last a light and fluffy roll, ready for spinning into yarn, the next step in the long transition from curly fleece to items such as clothing, blankets and rugs.

The rainbow is created by droplets in the air which break up white light into its component colors. It has many more than the six colors man's vision can detect. Insects see colors in the spectrum that we do not see.

COLOR PSYCHOLOGY
Rainbow in Your Mind

Louis Cheskin, a pioneer in the field of color psychology, is the Director of the Color Research Institute in Chicago, and a world-renowned authority on the subject. Stella Blum, Associate Curator of the Costume Department at the Metropolitan Museum in New York, is the author of a book on late 19th century costume. Mary Buckley, painter and sculptress, is Professor of Art at the Pratt Institute, New York and Instructor in the school's Department of Industrial Design.

Color is a complex and fascinating subject. A visual emotional cocktail, it has measurable, predictable effects on man, physiologically, psychologically, and emotionally. Although we don't know with certainty why people favor certain colors and color combinations, the fact that they do is the basis for a relatively new branch of study called color psychology. The term is a loose one covering a multitude of many kinds of investigation having to do with man and his responses to color, from how to keep him cheerful in a space capsule to how to persuade him to buy a can of coffee.

What Color Is

Color is a two-part (complementary) phenomenon involving the primary color components in light, or visible energy, and the primary colors in pigment, or matter. If all the colors in light are combined, the result is white light. If all the colors in pigment, or matter, are combined, the result is black, or the absence of light.

Each type (light or pigment) of color has a set of primary colors. The primaries the physicist works with—the primary colors of visible energy, light—are orange-red, green, and violet-blue. The physicists' secondaries (a combination of two primaries) are the primary colors of pigment, or matter— turquoise-blue, magenta-red, and yellow. The secondary colors of pigment are the primary colors of light. The color wheel shows these six hues.

What makes color even more complex is that primaries are not always classified in sets of three. Physiologists and psychologists list four primaries: red, green, yellow, and blue—the ones most people perceive as being independent of the influence of other colors. In color (process) printing, the pigment primaries are used. In color photography, the light primaries are involved or implemented as filters in primary color separation.

You can learn some things about color. Mix balanced, primary pigment colors to match those on the color wheel, and you will get black, which is the absence of light. Take three flashlights or projectors; in front of each, put a filter on one of the three light primaries, or physicist's primaries; project all three onto a screen, and the superimposed three colors will be white.

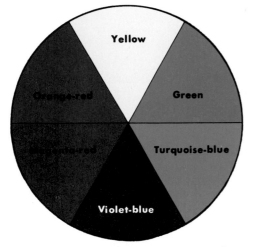

This color wheel shows the six basic colors, that the human eye perceives. They are divided into two groups: the physicist's primaries present in white light—orange-red, green, and violet-blue; and the pigment primaries, present in matter— turquoise-blue, magenta-red, and yellow.

Pigment primaries, turquoise-blue, magenta-red and yellow, combine in pairs to form the primaries of light: turquoise-blue and yellow make green; magenta-red and yellow make orange-red; magenta-red and turquoise-blue make violet-blue. All three pigment primaries, combined as shown here, make black.

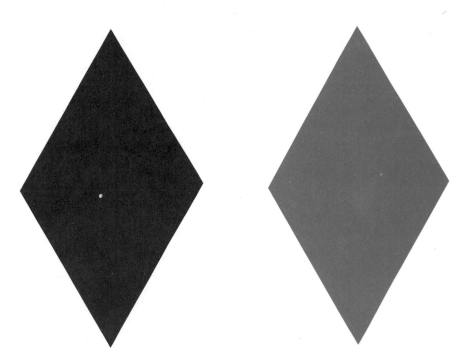

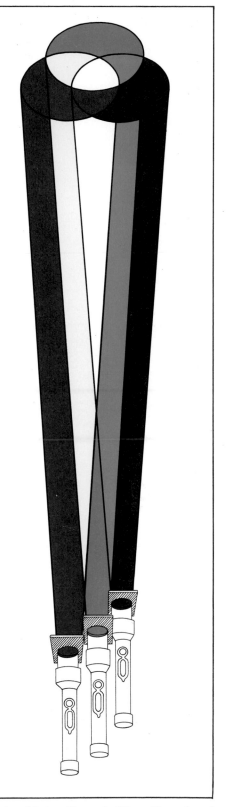

The power of after image: Stare at the diamonds for one minute in a bright light; then look at a blank white surface. You should see red and green reversed.

How We See Color

Show five friends the same red, and all will describe differently what they see. Their views are affected by countless factors, ranging from variations in sight to personal and cultural factors. Surrounding conditions—lighting, background colors, and perspective also affect the way you see a color. Human vision is believed by many scientists to respond to colors in pairs: one pair is black with white, while the others are the psychological primaries, red with green and blue with yellow. That the perception of color operates at least partly by pairing primaries is indicated by a phenomenon known as **after-image. It is illustrated by the diamonds above: Stare at the pair fixedly about 60 seconds; then shift your gaze to a blank white surface.** You will see the red and green reversed. The after image is the part of white light that has not saturated your eyes. If one of a pair of these colors is missing when you look at one color, your eyes will impose the image of the missing color if you look away to a white ground.

Dr. Louis Cheskin, Director of the Color Research Institute of America and one of the early researchers in color psychology, tells this story illustrating the effects of color pairing:

He was consulted by a paint manufacturer eager to produce paints in various colors for sale to farmers. The farmers had told him they were tired of traditional farm colors, ox-red and white, and bought them only because they were cheaper than other colors and also durable. Dr. Cheskin counseled the paint man to stick to ox-red and white for his farm market, because he believes that red satisfies a "red starvation" incurred from the endless green a farmer lives with in summer, while white has a conditioned association with cleanliness. The paint manufacturer went on with his plans for a range of colors. Eventually he turned to Dr. Cheskin and asked, "How did you know farmers wouldn't buy anything but red and white?"

The fact that we see colors in pairs apparently has other effects. It may account for some of the manifestations of color blindness. The most common color blindness is found in red/green perception, and one in 25 men have this to some degree, according to statistics of Helen Paulson, Research Psychologist at the U.S. Naval Base in New London, Conn. A man who is severely color defective in red/green perception sees purple, a combination of red and blue, as gray-blue. He sees greenish-yellow as gray-yellow because his eyes cannot receive the green wavelengths. The color test shown here is designed to

Lights, shining through filters the color of light primaries, project reflections of the pigment primaries where combinations of the light primaries—orange-red, green and violet-blue—overlap on the screen. Where all three of the light primaries overlap, white light is reflected.

501

reveal such inherited variances in color vision.

Insects, animals, and fish see differently. Most quadrupeds—for example, dogs and cats—are color blind. They see everything in a gray scale. What angers the bull is the movement of the matador's cloak, not the cloak's red color. Insects, whose vision equipment differs from ours, are believed to see part of the color spectrum the human eye cannot see.

Man's Response to Color

Man's reaction to color is both innate and learned. Innate responses are those born within us. Conditioned responses are those we have learned. The reasons behind innate responses to color are still unknown, but we do know that such responses to color exist. In fact, infants see color and respond to it before they see shapes. For example, red has great attention-getting power; it is stimulating. Normal children when presented a choice of a toy of several colors, will choose the red toy.

An experiment conducted by Dr. Cheskin in the 1930's and repeated by the Color Research Institute in Chicago in 1945, in an effort to measure innate response, placed people (with a medical attendant to measure physiological effects) in rooms of different colors, each totally a psychological primary. The rooms were duplicates in every other way—same exposure to light, same-size walls, same furnishings. In the red room, all large surfaces were red—

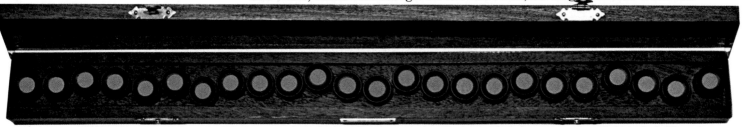

The Farnsworth-Munsell test to define color blindness consists of colored buttons arranged in a specific hue sequence from light to dark. The color-blind cannot correctly reproduce the sequence. The sequence here is one of the four sections of the test.

desks, walls, ceilings, floors, chairs. Some furnishings were of slightly different intensities of red—paper, pencils, other small objects. The other test rooms were exactly the same, but the colors were blue, yellow, and green.

The all-red room, Dr. Cheskin reported, measurably affected the subjects' nervous responses and pulse rate. Many couldn't stand the red room, couldn't bear to be in it. The all-blue room caused the pulse to slow and, again, drove many away. The all-yellow room blinded the subjects, and this reaction overshadowed the action of the pulse, which was erratic. No one could remain in the yellow room for even five minutes. The all-green room caused no physiological reactions, just an eagerness to get away from the intensities of a single color.

Dr. Cheskin says that doctors and physiologists with whom he discussed the experiment theorized that the subjects showed no pulse change in the green room because green is the color of nature, of growth, of accumulated energy from sunshine and, therefore, man's most comfortable environment.

Conditioned Responses to Color

While our need for color and our responses to the psychological primaries seem to be universal, in effect conditioned reactions and color associations differ. In Western culture, white is the symbol of purity and black of mourning, while in certain Eastern cultures of Asia, white is the symbol of mourning and black of purity.

Conditioned responses to color result from individual experiences associated with color and also from exposure to traditional uses of colors as symbols. American Indians used color to indicate direction. The selection varied from tribe to tribe. The Chippewa used red to represent the east; the Apache used black. The Sioux used blue for north; but to the Creek blue meant south. In

Hopi designs, yellow represents the north, green or blue the west, red the south, and white the east.

Ancient Greek color associations were of a different nature. Blue represented the earth and yellow the air. The Mesopotamians associated protection with colors. They wore blue to avert the evil eye; red amulets to promote healing; blue and violet to preserve faith and virtue; yellow to attract happiness and prosperity; green to induce fertility.

The medieval Catholic Church developed a color code for the illiterate and even quarreled with the Greek Orthodox Church about which branch of the church had the right to which color for which symbol. On statues and in paintings, the Roman Catholic code used red to denote charity, love and martyrdom; yellow for glory and power; green for immortality and faith; pale blue for peace and hope; white for purity; purple for sorrow; black for death.

From such historical uses of color, coupled with innate responses to color, we in the West associate red with fire, anger, love, hate; yellow with sunshine and cowardice; blue with calm, peace, depression, stagnation; green with nature, jealousy, inexperience. This color code is reflected in everyday speech. We talk of seeing red, feeling blue, turning green.

Color psychologists see color as both a key to personality and a tool for expressing or arousing emotions and behavior. Red is reported to be the choice of outgoing, extrovert personalities. It evokes warmth, excitement, rebellion, and strength. It is a stimulating color, and the presence of warm, red-tinged colors could help lift your spirits, warm your mood.

Deep blue is believed to denote calm, conformity, passivity, and retreat. Some of its shades seem to have a calming effect; but if you have a tendency to the blues, color psychologists usually recommend that you avoid using much blue in decoration.

Yellow is considered a relaxed, sunny, expansive color, representing optimism. Its presence in decoration has the cheering effect of sunlight.

Green is widely believed to express eagerness for growth and to be the most soothing of all the hues for decoration and the easiest to live with.

Man's Need for Color

A history of color in clothing suggests that we have a strong need for, and response to, color and new colors.

The first dyes were developed when man, having noticed that certain plants, insects, and stones left traces of color on objects, became skillful in obtaining coloring from natural sources. Ancient Egyptians derived blue pigment from powdered lapis lazuli; Central American Indians prized the cochineal beetle as a source of red; Colonial Americans grew indigo, a plant with blue flowers that yielded a blue dye, as a major crop for export.

As long as dyes depended on hard-to-come-by natural sources, unbleached fibers dominated dress, and exotic colors were the privilege of rank and, for a long time, its symbol. The Roman emperors wore robes colored with Tyrian purple, a valued dye obtained from tiny shellfish. (Emperor Aurelian refused to buy his wife a purple cloak because it was too expensive.) At one time, only China's emperor could wear a particular shade of yellow, the imperial color. To maintain the coupling of color with rank in the medieval period, sumptuary laws (those regulating extravagance on religious or moral grounds) restricted the use of colors to certain ranks or professions.

During the reign of Louis XV, new tints of light blue, violet, yellow, green, gray, and rose were developed. Adopted by his mistress, Madame de Pompadour, these colors influenced all those who came in contact with her, the artists who decorated her salons, the painters who depended on her for their livelihood, and the dressmakers who made her clothes.

With the invention of synthetic dyes in the nineteenth century, color became easily available, fabrics could be dyed strong pinks and blues, magentas, lavenders, and corals, and the new hues were quickly adopted by fashion. Though from then on color and privilege ceased to be associated, the use of color has increased with its availability.

CREDIT: SCALA NEW YORK/FLORENCE

The Emperor Justinian, ruler of Byzantium A.D. 527-565, wears a purple cloak to emphasize his rank in this striking mosaic in San Vitale, Ravenna, Italy. Dye was once so costly that only the rich could afford colorful fabrics. Eventually, purple became the prerogative of the emperor and his family. To wear the purple indicated noble status. The dye came from a shellfish called purpura, found off the coast of Tyre.

503

Blue distortion of color plate

Yellow distortion of color plate

Green distortion of color plate

Imagine yourself sitting down to a meal colored as these are, and you will understand the way in which color conditioning affects your eye and your appetite. These four pictures simulate a Color Research Institute experiment to test the effect of color on appetite. For the actual experiment, lights were played on the banquet table to color food in ways that it does not naturally appear.

The photograph above is a reproduction of familiar foods as close to their natural colors as four-color printing processes can approximate. The three photographs to the left have been distorted in the printing process to emphasize the blue, yellow and green in the color plates. To reconstruct a color photograph with inks printed on paper, as this one is, printers use only four colors—blue, red, yellow, and black—broken up into tiny dots and printed on top of each other in combinations that create the other colors you see here. If you look at this picture through a magnifying glass, you can see the dots of these four basic colors. The printed result represents, but cannot actually duplicate, reality. Your mind, knowing what steak *should* look like, helps you see these dots of ink as steak.

A printer's color bar, showing the four basic colors at full strength used to print the full-color reproductions in this book.

Of course, forces other than man's desire for color are at work in the color selections of any given era. At the time of the French Revolution, the country's patriotic fervor was expressed by the use of the tricolors of the French flag, red, white, and blue, in home decor and clothing.

How Color Psychology Is Used

Color psychologists all over the world have made an effort to disseminate color tests to coordinate information. Data is made available by such groups as the American Inter-Society Color Council and is put to a staggering array of uses. NASA applied color psychology to its space program, and the Navy used it in designing submarine interiors. The Post Office, the Presidential plane Air Force One, automobile factories, and many department stores, colleges, hospitals, and schools use what is known about color to convey dignity, authority, and integrity, to boost morale and hence production, to sell merchandise, to encourage study, to reassure, cheer, comfort.

A color psychologist's recommendations for a hospital might be like this: to welcome and calm anxiety, halls and entrances painted a warm, gentle apricot or peach; father-to-be waiting rooms in cool greens and blues to calm anxiety; stimulating orange-reds for physical-therapy areas; yellows to create cheer and optimism in convalescent rooms. Pink and peach in operation-recovery rooms reflect a healthy-looking color to the patient's skin and have a beneficial psychological effect.

Color association is an aspect of color psychology subject to much research. Marketing people use color association to sell products. The food we buy is often color-keyed—tinted, packaged, or illuminated to appeal to our color associations. Shoppers transfer the effect of the package to the product in the package. If a food is packaged in a color not usually associated with that food, it may not be appetizing. Would you be enthusiastic about drinking water that came out of the tap bright green?

In a famous experiment conducted by the Color Research Institute in 1946, a banquet was provided to test color's effect on appetite. During the banquet, lights that colored the food bizarrely were turned on. Many guests suddenly found that they could not eat. Some who continued to eat eventually felt ill. When the lighting returned to normal, appetites also returned.

Sometimes, however, we are protected from such uncomfortable feelings by our color memory—a habit that lets us see things as we expect to see them, despite changes in lighting conditions. If we own a blue car, for example, we are likely to see that car as blue even under lighting conditions that would make it difficult for anyone else to say what color it is.

Color association also affects our sense of taste. It is generally accepted that we can detect only sweet, salt, sour and bitter flavors, and that the rest of our identification of flavors is associated with our vision and our sense of smell. In another Color Research Institute test, consumers were shown coffee in cans of four different colors, asked to smell the contents and to rate them for aroma. Coffee in the blue can was judged by 79 percent of those tested as being mild; that in the red can by 84 percent as being rich; that in the yellow can by 87 percent as being bland; and that in the brown can by 73 percent as being strong. The coffee, of course, was identical in all four cans.

Color Psychology and Fashion

Color psychology research in the area of fashion suggests that the keys to color choice lie in personal vanity and in color associations. We often choose the colors of the season: in spring, the yellow of sunshine, the greens of sprouting leaves; in summer, flower colors and the light, whitened tints reflected by strong sunlight; in autumn, the browns of fading leaves; in winter, the reddened tones that suggest warmth. And we select colors that flatter our status. Black, often the color of mourning or of conservatism, as among the Puritans, is periodically rediscovered as a fashionable color for everything from formal evening wear to expensive lingerie.

For related projects see: "Leaded Glass," "Lighting Effects," "Oil Painting" "Watercolors."

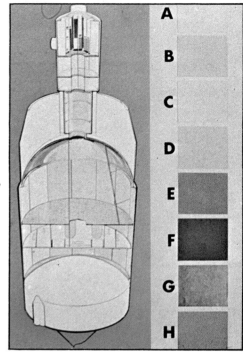

The interior of this lunar module was planned by color psychologists to use colors selected for beneficial associations as well as for light-reflective qualities and visual relief. The predominantly warm color scheme is keyed to the psychologically pleasing effect of light on skin tones and food. Since all sections of the capsule are areas in which the crew spent time, work as well as living spaces are colorful.

A. Light yellow: Walls, work area. Door wall, waste- and food-management area. Doors, sleep areas. Walls, half airlock-MDA.

B. Yellow-beige: Walls, sleep areas. Doors, food-management area. Walls, half airlock-MDA.

C. Light blue: Walls and doors, waste-management area.

D. Medium blue: Beds, sleep area.

E. Orange: Table and chair, food-management area.

F. Bright blue: Handrails.

G. Metallic gold: Floor and wall, grids. Screen vents, outer walls. Dome, upper tank section.

H. Dark yellow: Floors, food- and waste-management areas.

I: Off-white: Ceilings.

Sweet Tooth Recipes

Martin K. Hermann, candymaker for a quarter of a century, has worked at his complex art for confectioners all over the world. He now supervises a large confectionary in Portland, Ore. where he lives with his wife and two children. He is the author of The Art of Making Good Candies at Home, *published by Doubleday and Company.*

For youngsters, the making of candies is almost more fun than the eating. Choosing the recipe, measuring the ingredients, licking the beaters are the stuff from which some of the happiest childhood memories are made. True, candies are low-priority items with the calorie-counting adult; but when homemade, they are wholesome food and a good source of energy.

On the following pages, you will find recipes grouped in four categories: Quickie Candies, Hard Candies, Family Favorites, and Coated Chocolates.

Quickie Candies include comfits—fruits preserved or stuffed with various fillings—and this group that requires little or no cooking has some recipes suitable for young children to make. Hard Candies, with their high boiling temperatures, are best prepared by adults; but the giant lollipops made with the basic hard-candy formula delight children and are wonderful party gifts and decorations.

Family Favorites, which include the fudges and other popular sweets, require varying degrees of skill.

The Coated Chocolates (like those you buy in boxes of chocolates) are a challenge meant for the experienced cook.

These colorful and mouth-watering confections are all homemade. Clockwise from pink cherry cremes and green mint patties on pedestal stand: peanut brittle in covered glass jar; decorated, tinted glass lollipops; sugar-sanded jellies; almond toffee; rum-walnut candies; coconut balls; and hard candies. On the center tray, clockwise from the tinted glass hard candy: chocolate-almond toffee; chocolate-coated filbert-and-raisin clusters in footed bowl; toasted-coconut marshmallow; and assorted chocolate-dipped candies. Recipes are given on the following pages.

Vanessa Jansen helps her mother, Muriel,
put decorative touches on a fresh batch
of giant lollypops. (Recipe on page 509.)

1: Sprinkle ½ cup toasted coconut over the marshmallow. Let it set for 2 hours or overnight in a cool place.

2: Remove cooled marshmallow, with paper, from pan, and cut into squares. Dip knife in water to prevent sticking.

3: Soften the brown paper with a wet cloth, and peel it from the underside of the cut marshmallow squares.

4: Pull apart squares, and roll in the 2 cups coconut. Dry for 2 hours; then store in covered jar or cellophane bag.

Kitchen Favorites and Celebrations
Quickie candies

Toasted-Coconut Marshmallow

2 packages unflavored gelatin
⅔ cup cold water
1¼ cups granulated sugar
1 cup white corn syrup

½ to 1 teaspoon vanilla extract
½ teaspoon toasted-coconut flavoring
2½ cups toasted shredded coconut

Soften gelatin by stirring it into ⅓ cup cold water. Set aside. Boil sugar and remaining water about 2 minutes, until sugar dissolves. Wash down side of pot, as when making Hard Candy (photograph 5, opposite page), and bring to a boil. Pour this sugar syrup into a slightly warmed bowl. Add corn syrup and gelatin mixture; mix well. Beat at medium speed of electric beater until batch holds a good peak. When it rises over beaters, lift them a little so the tops show (this admits more air), and continue beating about 20 minutes. Stir in flavorings. Pour into brown-paper-lined, 8-by-12-by-2-inch baking pan; spread smooth to about 1¼ inches thick. For finishing, follow photographs 1 through 4. Makes 48 squares.

Quickie-Candy Basic Batch

1 tablespoon white corn syrup
⅔ cup sweetened condensed milk

4½ to 5 cups sifted confectioners' sugar

Pour syrup and milk into bowl; stir with wooden spoon while adding sugar gradually. If it gets too stiff to stir, put on waxed-paper baking sheet, and knead in rest of sugar. Should be like firm dough. Makes 5 cups.

Coconut Balls

1⅔ cups Quickie-Candy Basic Batch
¾ cup shredded white coconut

1 teaspoon coconut flavoring
1 teaspoon vanilla extract

Knead all ingredients, reserving ½ cup coconut. Roll into a rope, and slice into 1-inch pieces. Roll into balls in moistened hands; roll balls in reserved coconut on small plate. Makes 24 to 30.

Mint Patties

1⅔ cups Quickie-Candy Basic Batch
¼ teaspoon peppermint oil

4 drops green food color

Knead ingredients together. Roll into rope, and cut into ½-inch slices. Gently press into patties ¼ inch thick. Makes 35 to 40.

Cherry Cremes

1⅔ cups Quickie-Candy Basic Batch
1 teaspoon cherry flavoring
4 drops pink food color

¼ teaspoon citric acid, or 1 teaspoon lemon juice
20 candied cherries, halved

Knead all ingredients except cherries. Roll into rope; cut into 1-inch slices. Round these, and flatten slightly. Top each with cherry half. Makes 35 to 40.

Fruit Comfits

To make candied-citrus-peel comfits: Peel rind from orange, lemon, or grapefruit. Wash peel in cold water. Cut into ½-by-2-inch pieces. Boil in water to cover 30 minutes. Rinse in strainer under cold water; boil in fresh water 30 minutes more. Dry on paper towels; roll in granulated sugar. Dry at room temperature. To make stuffed-date comfits: Soak dried dates in orange juice, or rum. Remove pits. Fill each with marshmallow, walnut half, or 1 level teaspoon peanut butter. Reshape dates; roll in confectioners' sugar.

Kitchen Favorites and Celebrations
Hard candies

General Procedure

Put sugar, water, and corn syrup called for over medium heat, and stir as it heats. When it comes to a full boil for the first time, wash sugar crystals down from the sides of the pot (photograph 5), and add butter or margarine, if called for. Put candy thermometer in pot, and cook mixture without stirring until proper temperature—290F—is reached (photograph 6). Remove pot from stove, and add rest of ingredients, except citric acid, which must be folded into cooled batch on baking sheet.

Hard-Candy Drops

Basic batch for drop candies:

1 cup granulated sugar	4 drops flavoring of your choice
¼ cup water	Food color or paste (see below)
¼ cup corn syrup	

Follow the general procedure above. Then, from the tip of a teaspoon, drop small bits of hot mixture onto a greased baking sheet, without borders. To sand candies (sugarcoat them), place cooled pieces on damp towel so they are sticky, but not wet, all over, and roll in granulated sugar. Makes 30 pieces.

For cinnamon and mint drops, add cinnamon or mint flavoring to taste and 8 drops red or green color. For licorice drops, to the basic recipe add ¼ cup brown sugar, ¼ teaspoon anise flavoring, and 1 teaspoon black color paste. For butterscotch drops, to the basic recipe add ¼ cup brown sugar, 1 tablespoon butter or margarine, ½ teaspoon salt, and ¼ teaspoon butterscotch flavoring. Follow the procedure described above.

To make lollipops in various sizes, drop cooked hard-candy mix onto straws or wooden sticks (photograph 7). Decorate while hot and soft.

Sherry Jackson is very pleased with her lemon lollipop. It is decorated with small candy drops, taffy, and licorice.

Fruit-Flavor Candy Squares

For fruit-flavor hard candy, citric acid must be added after cooling. This makes the mixture too firm for drop candies, and reheating would destroy the citric acid and make the candies sticky. Instead of drops, make squares of fruit-flavor hard candy. Use the basic recipe for drop candies, and follow the general procedure above for making hard candy. Add appropriate flavoring and coloring (about 8 drops, yellow for lemon for example), and pour the cooked mixture onto a greased baking sheet. Let cool 2 minutes; then fold in ¼ teaspoon citric acid. Fold edges to make batch square. Flatten, and turn over. Score surface, while batch is still soft, with greased edge of a knife. Let cool; then break into pieces.

For large stained-glass panes, do not score or break candy; leave it whole.

5: After boiling hard-candy mix (see recipe above), wash down the sugar that clings to the side of the pot with a small, clean brush dipped in cold water.

6: Heat mix to 290F. Before this, test accuracy of your thermometer in boiling water. It should read 212F. If not, adjust cooking temperature accordingly.

7: Drop hard-candy mix on straws or wooden sticks to make lollipops. Decorate while hot and soft. Let stand to cool. Don't cool them in the refrigerator.

Kitchen Favorites and Celebrations
Family favorites

Penuche

3 cups light-brown sugar, firmly packed
1 cup light cream
2 tablespoons white corn syrup
2 tablespoons butter
1 teaspoon vanilla extract
1 cup chopped nuts

Combine sugar, cream, and corn syrup in a medium saucepan. Over medium heat, cook, stirring constantly, to 236F on candy thermometer, or until a little of the mixture dropped in cold water forms a soft ball. Remove from heat; drop in butter. Do not stir. Cool to 110F, or until lukewarm. Add vanilla. Beat until mixture loses its gloss and a small amount dropped from a spoon will hold its shape. Stir in nuts. Pour into lightly buttered 8-by-8-by-2-inch pan. Let cool; then cut into squares. Makes about 1½ pounds.

Chocolate Fudge

2 cups granulated sugar
⅛ teaspoon salt
¾ cup light cream
2 squares bittersweet chocolate, grated
2 tablespoons butter
1 teaspoon vanilla extract
⅔ cup chopped walnuts

Cook as for Penuche, above. Makes a little more than 1 pound.

Almond Toffee

1 cup toasted chopped almonds
1½ cups granulated sugar
¼ cup water
⅓ cup corn syrup
½ pound butter
½ teaspoon salt
¼ teaspoon baking soda

Warm almonds in 175F oven, and keep warm. Put sugar, water, and corn syrup in pot, and stir over medium heat until mixture boils. Wash sugar crystals down from side of pot (see photograph 5, page 509). Keep boiling. Stir in butter until it is completely melted. Put candy thermometer into pot, and cook mixture to 290F; stir constantly. Remove from heat, and add salt, baking soda, and warm almonds. Reheat 1 minute. Pour onto greased baking sheet, and spread evenly to about ¼ inch thick. Score into ½-by-1-inch pieces. Let cool. When batch feels plastic, like caramel, turn it over by running a spatula beneath it. When fully cooled, break along score lines. If you wish, coat on all sides with tempered chocolate (see page 512) and 1½ cups toasted chopped almonds. Cool near open window for a few moments only. Makes 35 to 40 pieces.

Peanut brittle and filbert brittle look inviting in a clear-glass bowl. Cashew or Brazil nuts can also be used. (Brittle recipe is on the opposite page.)

8: With a knife, score almond toffee into ½-by-1-inch rectangles. Let it stand at room temperature to cool. Do not refrigerate; it would get sticky.

9: After almond toffee has been broken into pieces, it may be dipped into a pot of tempered chocolate and then rolled in a tray of toasted chopped almonds.

Pieces of marshmallow rolled in toasted coconut and coated with chocolate. On this page is the recipe for Rocky Road, another marshmallow confection.

Filbert or Peanut Brittle

1 cup granulated sugar
¼ cup water
¼ cup corn syrup
2 tablespoons butter or margarine

½ to ¾ cup raw filberts or raw,
    shelled Spanish peanuts
½ teaspoon salt
¼ teaspoon baking soda
¼ teaspoon vanilla extract

Put sugar, water, and corn syrup in pot; stir over medium heat until it boils. With wooden spoon, wash sugar crystals down from side of pot. Stir in butter. Cook to 260F on candy thermometer, without further stirring. Then stir in nuts, and cook, stirring gently with thermometer, to 310F. Remove from heat. Add salt, baking soda, and vanilla. Spread on greased baking sheet. Cool slightly; then turn it over with a long knife, and stretch it as thin as possible. Cool at room temperature until hard and brittle. Break into pieces, and store in container to keep out moisture. Makes 35 to 40 pieces.

Rocky Road

1 batch marshmallow
½ cup flour, sifted

3 cups tempered chocolate
½ cup chopped walnuts

Make marshmallow (page 508) without coconut or flavoring. Cover batch in pan with flour, and roll in flour instead of coconut. Brush off excess; let dry 2 hours. Temper chocolate (page 512); rewarm slightly by holding baking sheet 1 foot above low heat until bottom feels warm. Stir again; gently stir in marshmallow and nuts. Pour into 8-by-8-inch baking pan lined with waxed paper or foil; spread about 1½ inch thick. Cool. Cut off any to be eaten soon. Wrap rest in foil; it will stay fresh for weeks.

Kitchen Favorites and Celebrations
Coated chocolates

Making coated chocolates is challenging and fun. Ingredients are the filling —such as toffee or ginger squares, marshmallow, cremes, peanuts, filberts, and raisins—and the tempered chocolate in which they are dipped. To coat 2 cups of filling pieces, such as toffee, I work with 4 cups (2 pounds) of tempered chocolate. But 1 cup of tempered chocolate will coat 1 cup of smaller pieces, such as peanuts, filberts, or raisins.

Chocolate for coating is available in pieces or pound bags at candy plants and often at local markets. Store chocolate in a cool, dry place but not the refrigerator. Melt 2 pounds of chocolate coating, cut in small pieces, in a double-boiler top over hot water. The water should be no hotter than 140F or chocolate will form grainy lumps. Stir occasionally with a dry spoon. Work in a cool room (65 to 68F) or near an open window. While chocolate is melting, use a cheese grater to grate ¼ pound chocolate into a fine dust. This is seeding chocolate (see below). Set aside. Pour ⅔ of melted chocolate onto a clean, dry baking sheet. (Wipe bottom of pot before you pour; even one drop of water in the chocolate would make it too thick for dipping.) With short, quick motions of a steel spatula, spread chocolate on baking sheet from sides to center and back again, to cool it (photograph 10). Continue until chocolate feels neither warm nor cool when dabbed on your wrist (85 to 90F). Then sprinkle 1 heaping teaspoon of seeding chocolate on cooled chocolate; mix thoroughly with spatula. This will seed the chocolate coating with unmelted cocoa-butter crystals and help it set properly.

During dipping, chocolate must be at about 90F. Work with baking sheet on a towel to keep the bottom from cooling. Place filling piece upside down in chocolate so that ⅔ of it is submerged. Use a fork to ladle chocolate over filling, coating it completely. Move the fork back over the piece to wipe off surplus chocolate. Lift the piece from the chocolate; then lower it onto the surface of the chocolate two or three times, touching it only lightly. This pulls surplus chocolate from sides of piece. Flip piece over onto waxed paper. If chocolate runs off sides, not enough was wiped off, or chocolate was too warm, or there was not enough seeding chocolate in it. If chocolate gets too cool and thick for dipping, mix in a little of remaining ⅓ warm chocolate.

To make nut and raisin clusters, mix a cupful with 1 cupful of tempered chocolate. Spoon bite-size clusters onto a sheet of wax paper (photograph 11) or shape into patties (see photograph page 506). Cool pieces at room temperature, or cool in the refrigerator for no longer than 15 minutes.

For related projects, see the entries "Birthday Celebrations," "Christmas Celebrations," "Marmalades, Jams, Jellies," and "Spun-Sugar Cookery."

Homemade chocolate-coated candied ginger and nut clusters look just like those you buy—but always seem to taste better.

10: Tempering melted chocolate with a spatula. Well-tempered-chocolate coating has a satin-like sheen when cooled.

11: Using two spoons to move nut clusters from the coating batch of tempered chocolate to a sheet of waxed paper.